A FRIENDLY GUIDE TO

THE BOOK OF REVELATION

FRANCIS J MOLONEY

Published in Australia by
Garratt Publishing
32 Glenvale Crescent
Mulgrave, VIC 3170
www.garrattpublishing.com.au

Text copyright © Francis J. Moloney 2020
All rights reserved. Except as provided by the Australian copyright law, no part of this book may be reproduced in any way without permission in writing from the publisher.

Design and typesetting by Lynne Muir
Images copyright © iStock; Wikipedia

Scripture quotations are drawn from the New Revised Standard Version of the Bible, copyright © 1989 by the Division of Christian Education of the National Council of the Churches of Christ in the USA.

Used by permission.
All rights reserved.

Nihil Obstat: Reverend Monsignor Peter Kenny STD, Diocesan Censor, Catholic Archdiocese of Melbourne
Imprimatur: Very Reverend Joseph Caddy, AM, Lic. Soc. Sci VG, Vicar General, Catholic Archdiocese of Melbourne
Date: 21 July 2020
The Nihil Obstat and Imprimatur are official declarations that a book or pamphlet is free of doctrinal or moral error. No implication is contained therein that those who have granted the Nihil Obstat and Imprimatur agree with the contents, opinions or statements expressed. They do not necessarily signify that the work is approved as a basic text for catechetical instruction.

ISBN 9 781925 073157

Cataloguing in Publication information for this title is available from the National Library of Australia.
www.nla.gov.au

The author and publisher gratefully acknowledge the permission granted to reproduce the copyright material in this book. Every effort has been made to trace copyright holders and to obtain their permission for the use of copyright material.

The publisher apologises for any errors or omissions in the above list and would be grateful if notified of any corrections that should be incorporated in future reprints or editions of this book.

IN MEMORY OF PROFESSOR EUGENIO CORSINI (1924–2018)

CONTENTS

Preface **3**

Introduction **4**

The Prologue and the Letters: Rev 1:1–3:22 **22**

The Opening of the Seven Seals: Rev 4:1–8:1 **27**

The Blowing of the Seven Trumpets: Rev 8:2–11:19 **35**

Preparation for the Pouring Out of the Seven Bowls: Rev 12:1–14:20 **41**

The Pouring Out of the Seven Bowls: Rev 15:1–16:21 **46**

Consequences of the Pouring Out of the Seven Bowls: Rev 17:1–22:5 **51**

The Epilogue: Rev 22:6–21 **57**

A Final Word **60**

Glossary **61**

Endnotes and Bibliography **64**

Cover: *The Angel with the Little Scroll*
"The mystery of God will be fulfilled" (Rev 10:7)

Title page: *Death on a Pale Horse* by Joseph Mallory Turner

Page 3: The Anastasis fresco in the Church of the Holy Saviour in Chora, by Jose Luiz Bernardes Ribeiro

PREFACE

The *Friendly Guide* series has made a significant contribution to biblical education. Books on the Prophets; the New Testament; the Gospels of Mark, Matthew, Luke and John; the figure of the Apostle Paul; Women in the Bible; and other biblically based themes have appeared. Since the Encyclical *Providentissimus Deus* of Pope Leo XIII in 1893, the teaching authority of the Catholic Church has insisted on the central role the Word of God in our Christian lives and liturgies. Pope Francis has recently established the Second Sunday of Ordinary Time as a day for the whole Church to celebrate the Word of God each year. The time is ripe for a more widespread and deep knowledge of our Sacred Scriptures.

But a *Friendly Guide to the Book of Revelation* is a challenge! There have always been doubts about the meaning and relevance of Revelation. Eastern Churches do not hold it in high regard. Martin Luther (1483–1546), writing a preface to Revelation for his German version of the New Testament, complained: "I can in no way detect that the Holy Spirit produced it … There are many far better books available for us to keep" (1522). Fundamentalist Christians read the narratives as signs of the end of time, applying the book's symbols to the evils of their times – from a corrupt Catholic Church in the sixteenth century, to the contemporary COVID–19 pandemic – as God's angry punishment of sinful humankind.

The key to the interpretation that follows is a recognition that Revelation is about the perennial presence of the saving effects of "the Lamb slaughtered from the foundation of the world" (Rev 13:8). It depends upon two recently published studies: my full-scale commentary on Revelation: *The Apocalypse of John. A Commentary* (Grand Rapids: Baker Academic, 2020) and my guide through its use in the Church's liturgies: *Reading Revelation at Easter Time* (Collegeville: Liturgical Press, 2020). I trust that this *Friendly Guide* shows that, as conflict rages between good and evil, Revelation is an inspired reflection upon the definitive victory of God in Jesus' death and resurrection.

It is dedicated to the memory of Professor Eugenio Corsini of the University of Turin (1924–2018). His personal influence and ground-breaking work lie behind almost everything that follows.

Francis J. Moloney, SDB, AM, FAHA

INTRODUCTION

A FRIENDLY GUIDE TO A HOSTILE BOOK

Apocalyptic literature appeared in an early form in the Old Testament (e.g., Ezekiel, Isaiah 24–27, Zechariah, and especially Daniel). It developed among Jewish authors into a major way of writing in times of trouble (e.g., 1 Enoch, 4 Ezra, 2 Baruch and some texts from the Dead Sea Scrolls). There are also Christian apocalypses (e.g., 5 Ezra, Sibylline Oracles and Shepherd of Hermas). [1]

Below: *The Last Judgement* **in the Duomo, Florence**

Right: The Wailing Wall, Jerusalem

Most would claim that it is impossible to render the Book of Revelation "friendly". Given the anger and violence that it has inspired over the centuries, especially among Christians, it could better be described as "hostile".

THE CHALLENGE OF READING REVELATION

The book is heavily dependent upon earlier writings from the Jewish Scriptures (our Old Testament). They belong to what is called an "apocalyptic" form of literature. Indeed, picking up the very first Greek word of the text (*apocalypsis*), the Book of Revelation is often called "the Apocalypse". The Greek word means "unveiling," or "revelation", i.e., making known or visible. The modern name "the Book of Revelation" is a translation of the first Greek word of the book.

In general terms, apocalyptic literature appeared within Judaism when Israel found itself under threat of destruction. The authorities and people were powerless. Israel's evil enemies were so dominant that the nation's imminent political destruction was inevitable. The destruction of the temple and the religious life and practices of the nation would follow. Authors wrote narrative theological reflections promising that God would enter the story, destroy the wicked and save the virtuous. What was humanly impossible would be achieved through the direct intervention of God. John of Patmos, a Jewish-Christian who authored the book

INTRODUCTION

of Revelation (Rev 1:1, 4, 9; 22:8) used Israel's Scriptures to find his language and imagery. He *never* cites the name of the biblical book he is using. Among all his allusions to Israel's Scriptures, John's favourites were the prophets Ezekiel and Daniel. Ezekiel appeared during the time of Israel's exile in Babylon (586–539 BCE). Daniel opposed the efforts of the Seleucid King Antiochus IV (175–164 BCE) to force Israel to accept the ways of the Greeks by military means. He desecrated the Jerusalem temple in 169 BCE.

But once the God of Israel becomes the main agent of the story, symbolic language, and descriptions of unimaginable and fierce sequences of events are used. God's entry into history could not be paralleled with human processes. At the time John was writing Revelation, many Jewish apocalypses, and even Christian apocalypses, appeared, following the destruction of Israel and its Temple, results of the Jewish revolt against Roman authority in 65–70 CE. **(see box far left)**.

The puzzling symbols and violent narrative sequences of apocalyptic literature indicated a God who transcends the human story. The Lord of history acted on Israel's behalf. John makes copious use of such symbols and narrative sequences. As we will see, *he uses them in his own unique fashion.* Encountering these descriptions, as they appear in the Book of Revelation, we find ourselves "outside" the world in which apocalyptic language was current. Unless we have a key that allows us entry into this challenging worldview, John's book remains a puzzle for contemporary Christians.

KEY NOTES

◆ "Revelation" is an English translation of the Greek word *apocalypsis,* which also means "unveiling".

◆ As well as Revelation, there are other biblical books in the Old Testament, in Jewish literature and in early Christian literature that use the same symbolic language and stories.

◆ To ask people to wait patiently in suffering, and even martyrdom, in the hope that God will finally destroy evil and reward good is hardly Christian.

◆ Violence is widespread in Jewish apocalyptic literature.

INTRODUCTION

> **WHAT ARE WE WAITING FOR?**
> You are worthy to take the scroll and to open its seals, for you were slaughtered and by your blood you ransomed for God saints from every tribe and people and nation; you have made them to be a kingdom and priests serving our God and they will reign on earth.
> Rev 5:9–10

Right: *Dragon menaces woman* by Giusto de Menabuoi

Is Revelation Christian?

We Christians of the third Christian millennium face a more subtle problem. The basic presupposition of a Jewish apocalypse is that *in the end* God will overcome all evil, punish and destroy it, and reward the faithful. The message of apocalyptic literature is essentially associated with "the end". In technical language, we call it "eschatological". This word means that it tells a story of God's *final* solution of an insurmountable human problem.

Is this Christian? Does the inspired Word of God found in Revelation, part of the Christian Bible for almost two thousand years, ask us to endure all the suffering, rejection, abuse, and martyrdom of our present age because in the end God will sort it out?

Does Revelation mysteriously prophesy the suffering and death that accompanies the spread of the COVID–19 pandemic? Is this "plague" a sign of God's just anger? If so, does this lessen the significance of the role of self-sacrificing and heroic medical personnel, and the work of governments to protect their people? Of course not. Christian history teaches us, however, that theological fanaticism lurks behind many readings of Revelation.

In a Christian view of history, something new has entered the human story in the life and teaching, death and resurrection of Jesus Christ. John makes it clear on the very first page of Revelation that Jesus Christ has made a difference. He greets the churches in Asia with a word from God "and from Jesus Christ, the faithful witness, the firstborn from among the dead, and the ruler of the kings of the earth" (1:5). John describes Jesus Christ as the one "who loves us and freed us by his blood, and made us to be a kingdom, priests serving his God and Father" (1:6; see 5:9–10). What, then, are we waiting for?

What is the Book of Revelation?

The Book of Revelation, found at the end of a printed Bible, has fascinated and puzzled Christians for centuries. With such vivid imagery as the four horsemen (Rev 6:1–9), the Beast whose number is 666 (13:18), and the battle at Harmagedon (16:12–21), many wrongly see it as a map to the end of the world. This well-established interpretation is at everyone's fingertips on Google and in various entries in Wikipedia. This *Friendly Guide* will endorse a different understanding of Revelation. It is a book that uses end-time language to proclaim the victory of God over evil in the death and resurrection of Jesus Christ.

INTRODUCTION

Quick outline of Revelation

John's use of "sevens" shapes the book's argument, framed by a prologue and an epilogue.

John's prologue: greetings and introduction (1:1–8)
- A heavenly encounter and the letters to seven churches (1:9–3:22)
- A heavenly encounter and the opening of the seven seals (4:1–8:1)
- A heavenly encounter and the blowing of the seven trumpets (8:2–11:19)
    - A threefold preparation for the pouring out of the seven bowls: the woman and the dragon (12:1–18), the two beasts (13:1–18) and God's initial intervention (14:1–20)
- A heavenly encounter and the pouring out of the seven bowls (15:1–16:21)
    - The threefold consequences of the pouring out of the seven bowls: the destruction of Babylon (17:1–19:10), the destruction of all evil powers (19:11–21:8), and the gathering of the faithful in the New Jerusalem (21:9–22:5)

John's epilogue: greetings and conclusion (22:6–21)

INTRODUCTION

THE BOOK OF REVELATION AT A GLANCE

CHAPTER 1:1–8	CHAPTER 1:9–20	CHAPTER 2	CHAPTER 3	CHAPTER 4	CHAPTER 5
John's greeting and prologue	Heavenly encounter	Letters to churches at Ephesus, Smyrna, Pergamum, and Thyatira	Letters to churches at Sardis, Philadelphia, and Laodicea	Heavenly encounter 1: vision of the court of the creator	Heavenly encounter 2: vision of the redeeming Lamb
CHAPTER 6	**CHAPTER 7:1–8:1**	**CHAPTER 8:2–13**	**CHAPTER 9**	**CHAPTER 10**	**CHAPTER 11**
Opening of the first six seals	Opening of the sixth seal finalised, and the opening of the seventh seal	Heavenly encounter 8:7–13: blowing of the first four trumpets and preparation for the "woes"	Blowing of the fifth and sixth trumpets: two "woes"	Blowing of the sixth trumpet continues	Blowing of the sixth trumpet finalised and the blowing of the seventh trumpet: the third "woe"
CHAPTER 12	**CHAPTER 13**	**CHAPTER 14**	**CHAPTER 15**	**CHAPTER 16**	**CHAPTER 17**
The first preparation for the pouring out of the bowls: the woman and the dragon	The second preparation for the pouring out of the bowls: the two beasts	The third preparation for the pouring out of the bowls: the salvation of the faithful in Israel	Heavenly encounter	The pouring out of the seven bowls: Harmagedon	First consequence of the pouring out of the bowls: the destruction of Babylon
CHAPTER 18	**CHAPTER 19:1–10**	**CHAPTER 19:11–21**	**CHAPTER 20**	**CHAPTER 21:1–22:5**	**CHAPTER 22:6–21**
The destruction of Babylon continued	The rejoicing of the saints as Babylon is humiliated. The end of the first consequence of the pouring out of the bowls.	The second consequence: the rider of the white horse destroys the beast and its armies	The final battle, the thousand-year reign, the defeat of Satan. The end of the second consequence.	The third consequence: the vision of the heavenly Jerusalem and the gathering of the faithful	John's epilogue and farewell

INTRODUCTION

Who wrote the Book of Revelation?

The author tells us that his name is John (1:1, 4, 9; 22:8). He was not the author of the Fourth Gospel. His profound knowledge of the Hebrew Scriptures, used at every turn of his book, shows that he was Jewish. This impression is supported by the author's use of the Greek language in his book. Although very powerful, it is unique in its rough expression and the steady presence of grammatical errors. The Book of Revelation is the work of a Jew, writing in a language that was not his mother tongue.

He must have been well known to some of the Christian churches in Asia (today's Western Turkey) as he addresses his letters to seven of them (2:1–3:22). He tells us that he is writing from the island of Patmos, just off the coast of Turkey.

Patmos was never a Roman penal settlement. John is there "because of the word of God and the testimony of Jesus" (1:9). Despite popular opinion (e.g. Google and Wikipedia), he was not a prisoner, but a passionate missionary who proclaimed God's word and what God has done for us through the death and resurrection of Jesus.

What is Revelation about?

An otherwise unknown figure, named John, wrote to the Church in Asia, symbolised by seven churches, about God's victory over evil in and through the death and resurrection of Jesus.

After a prologue, in which John indicates that there are

Above: St John by Alonso Cano (1601 — 1667)

Below: Saint John the Evangelist monastery at Patmos island, Greece

INTRODUCTION

two moments in God's saving presence: the time of Israel and the time of the Christian Church (1:1–8), he uses a series of "sevens" to communicate his message. Each of the sevens begins with a heavenly encounter during which someone is commissioned. John is authorised to communicate letters to seven fragile churches (1:9–20). The slain yet risen Lamb is authorised to open the seven seals of a scroll that no one else in heaven could open (4:1–5:14). Seven angels are commissioned to blow seven trumpets (8:2–6). Seven angels are commissioned to pour out seven bowls (15:1–8).

The dictation of the letters (2:1–3:22), the opening of the seals (6:1–8:1), the blowing of the trumpets (8:7–11:19) and the pouring out of the bowls (16:1–21) all tell of fierce encounters between the powers of evil and the powers of good. In each case it appears that evil is rampant and victorious – at least over part of humankind and God's creation. But by the end of each series of seven, that situation has been reversed: God is victorious (3:20; 6:12–8:1; 11:15–19; 16:12–21). Each "seven" intensifies this message, until the announcement of the Battle of Harmagedon in 16:12–21. Two aspects of that battle are further described in 19:17–21 and 20:7–10. All evil powers (19:17–21) and Satan

Above: *The Beast with the Seven Heads,* **from Battistero di Padova**

and his entourage (20:7–10) are defeated.

To highlight God's action in the salvation of humankind, the final "seven" (the pouring out of the bowls) is *prepared for* by three visions. John sees the human situation in the encounter between the woman and the dragon (12:1–18), the agents of Satan in the two beasts (13:1–18) and God's initial saving action for the saints of Israel (14:1–20). These preparations are matched by a threefold report of the *consequences* of Harmagedon that follow the pouring out of the bowls. John reports the destruction of Babylon (17:1–19:10), the destruction of all evil powers (19:11–21:8), and the gathering of the faithful in the New Jerusalem (21:9–22:5). He

then closes his book with an epilogue (22:6–21).

The use of "seven" is a symbol of completeness. The seven churches of Asia are failing in various ways, giving in to the corruption of the Greco-Roman world (2:1–3:22). They receive recommendations for the whole Church, and the victors against corruption will be blessed. They reflect a struggling and fragile Church. In the New Jerusalem a temple is no longer needed because God and the Lamb dwell there. It portrays the Church as it should be (21:9–22:5).

John looks back across the whole of human history and portrays the presence of evil through the end-time symbols of violent horses and their riders (6:1–8), locusts that sting like scorpions (9:1–11), dragons (12:1–18), beasts from the sea and from the land (13:1–18), huge and powerful armies (9:13–19), heavenly and earthly disasters (e.g. 6:12–17; 8:4–5; 11:19), and many other powerful images and symbols. Evil brings pain and suffering but not repentance and conversion (6:15–17; 9:20–21; 16:8–9, 10–11, 21; 18:4; 21:2–8, 27; 22:11, 14–15). That situation has been transformed by the death and resurrection of Jesus. Still using violent end-time language, John portrays a definitive battle between good and evil at

INTRODUCTION

Harmagadon (16:12–21). God is victorious over evil, destroying its agents (19:17–21), and locking down Satan and his cohorts (20:7–10).

Evil persists, as we all know, but because of Jesus' death and resurrection, we live in the New Jerusalem. All of this has "suddenly" transformed the human story. John asks his readers of all time: take stock of yourselves. Where do you belong? In the New Jerusalem of the sacrificed Lamb, or outside, selling out to the more immediate gratification of the status quo?

Text style

Revelation is very different from the other books in the New Testament, but it is full of imagery and symbols that John has taken from what he regarded as the Word of God: the Sacred Scriptures of Israel. He is especially fond of Ezekiel and Daniel. But he also uses or alludes to many other Old Testament passages. In his unique way, however, he never cites the sources or the authors of the passages he uses so powerfully. In our printed Bibles, and in most of the earliest manuscripts of the New Testament, Revelation appears as the final book in the collection. It is a challenging conclusion!

Despite its popularity, even in

Above: Kronheim's Baxter process illustration of Revelation 22:17 (King James' Version)

today's social media, an end-time interpretation misses John's point. It is true that John makes continual use of *apocalyptic* writing. But he does not use it to point to the imminent arrival of the end time. For him, it portrays the destructive power of evil, but the even more powerful presence of God's victory in and through Jesus Christ. It is not used to focus the audience's attention on *the imminent future*, something that will happen "soon", but to instruct believers about the "sudden" intervention of God *in the past* and the need for a confident community of believers *in the present* because of that intervention. God will intervene "quickly", but we do not know when.

The Greek expression *tachos/tachus* (1:1; 2:16; 3:11; 11:14; 22:6, 7, 12, 20) can mean both "soon" and "quickly". Contrary to most interpretations, our *Friendly Guide* claims that John insists upon the nature of God's final intervention ("quickly"), not its timing ("soon").

The document is full of references to God's victory in the messianic enthronement of the Lamb slain and risen, to free humankind from evil (5:6, 9–14; 7:12–8:1; 11:15–19; 16:17–21; 18:20–24; 19:1–8, 17–21; 20:11–15; 21:1–22:5). The "saints" were not persecuted Asian Christians, as has long been argued. Under the influence of Daniel, they are those from Israel's history who lived by the word of God and accepted the messianic witness of the prophets (Dan 7. See Rev 8:3–4; 11:18; 13:7, 10; 14:12; 16:6; 17:6; 18:20, 24; 19:8; 20:6, 9). They already have life, the application of the saving effects of the death and resurrection of the Lamb "from the foundation of the world" (13:8). "Over these the second death [i.e., the final judgment] has no power" (20:6).

Historical background

Contemporary studies of the background that produced Revelation lie behind the interpretation of this *Friendly Guide*. We must start from

INTRODUCTION

a more accurate assessment of the historical situation in Roman Asia that motivated the writing of the book. It has long been maintained that the book was written in a time of severe Roman persecution of Christians, and the threatening imposition of Emperor worship. Many early writers, both Roman and Christian, claimed that the Emperor Domitian (81–96 CE) instigated an Empire-wide systematic persecution of Christians. For centuries, Christian interpreters have taken this claim for granted. Historians are now almost unanimous in claiming that things did not happen like that!

There seems to have been an early brief and brutal persecution in the time of the Emperor Nero (54–68 CE). But scholars also doubt if this was as focused upon Christians as has been later claimed by both Roman and Christian writers. There was no systematic persecution of Asian Christians at the end of the first Christian century.

Persecution of Christians became a major feature of the later centuries, as the spread of the Christian religion appeared to threaten Roman authority and religion, including Emperor worship. This was a regular feature of the third century and closed with fierce persecutions early in the fourth century. From approximately 112 CE, we have a correspondence between with the Emperor Trajan (98–117 CE) and Pliny the Younger (61–113 CE), the Governor of Bithynia-Pontus (modern Turkey). Pliny seeks the Emperor's advice on how he should go about performing the legal investigation of Christians. This is the first Roman document that mentions Christians, written well after the Book of Revelation (96 CE). It is clear there was no Roman "policy" on the treatment of Christians some 15 years after John wrote his book. The correspondence between Trajan and Pliny shows that such a policy would soon be called for.

Later Christian writers (e.g. Irenaeus [c. 130–c. 202 CE], Eusebius [c. 260–c. 340 CE] and Augustine [354–430 CE]) anachronistically read the later persecutions of Christians back into the first century, turning Domitian into a monster. They saw the suffering and death of a Domitian persecution as the inspiration of John's writing to Christians who were wavering in such challenging circumstances.

Below: *St John on Isle of Patmos*, wood engraving, published 1886

INTRODUCTION

On the evidence of these great figures from the Church's early centuries, Roman persecution has long been considered the background for the Book of Revelation.

Similarly, Emperor worship was widespread throughout the Empire by the end of the first Christian century. It became closely associated with the persecution and execution of Christians in later centuries. But there is little or no evidence that Christians were being forced to take an active role in pagan cults or suffer persecution and death at the end of the first century. In sum, things were peaceful in Asia as John was writing his book, although the demand for Christians to worship the Emperor was certainly present later in the second century.

In recent times, a more critical reading of the historical background to the Book of Revelation has led to alternative interpretations. They question the traditional view that the book was written to comfort suffering Christians by pointing to God's victory at the end of time. In the traditional understanding of the historical background to Revelation as the experience of suffering and death at the hands of the Roman authorities, John asked his audience to persevere in suffering. His use of end-time language and its promises encouraged them that God would destroy the evil and reward the virtuous *at the end of time.*

A more accurate understanding of the historical background that produced John's work, as briefly outlined previously, necessarily calls

KEY NOTES

- John uses end-time language and symbols, but he applies them to the destructive effects of evil, and the signs of God's victory in Jesus' death and resurrection.

- This practice makes John's book different from all other examples of apocalyptic literature.

- The Book of Revelation was widely known, but had difficulty in being accepted as part of the Christian Scriptures.

- We are not the first Christians to have difficulty in finding something useful for our faith-lives in the Book of Revelation.

Below: *The Last Angel* **by Nicholas Roerich, Moscow 1942**

INTRODUCTION

Above: Daniel by Michelangelo from the Sistine Chapel

Right: Stained glass in the Church of Tervuren, Belgium, depicting a burning lamb, symbolizing the Agnus Dei

GOD'S VICTORY OVER EVIL
The seventh angel poured his bowl into the air, and a loud voice came out of the temple, from the throne, saying, "It is done!"

JESUS CHRIST'S FINAL COMING
The one who testifies to these things says, "Surely I am coming quickly." Amen. Come, Lord Jesus (22:20).

for newer interpretations. If Christianity had disappeared from the face of the earth at the end of the first century, no one would have noticed the difference. There was no conflict between Rome and Christianity at that time. Revelation is not primarily concerned about Rome or Emperor worship. Nor is it a book exhorting suffering Christians to persevere in their faith in the face of persecution as they wait for the imminent victory of God *at the end of time.*

The Book of Revelation is not an anti-Roman document, although Rome is certainly in view when John describes the powers of evil. Rome is the most recent "empire" to combine corrupt political authority and corrupt religious authority to establish a destructive sinful society. John's book looks back across the whole of the history of Israel. Evil has always been rampant.

John's favourite book, Daniel, tells the story of Israel's enemies, beginning with its supposed setting in the court of Nebuchadnezzar in sixth-century BCE Babylon, through allusions to other "empires", down to the Hellenistic invasion and destruction of Antiochus IV (175–164 BCE). For John and his audience, the Romans belong to this long history of rejection of the one true God. The Roman Empire happens to be the current evil power. It continues to represent a long history of evil that has oppressed humankind from the beginnings of time. All such evil has been defeated by God in and through the death and resurrection of Jesus Christ.

John addresses late first-century Asian Christians, presenting the model of the "saints" who have been saved by the blood of the Lamb "from the foundation of the world" (13:8). They lived by the word of God and accepted the messianic promises of the prophets. Such "saints" offer the Asian Christians encouragement and hope as they are tempted by the allure of the Greco-Roman world and its practices. John invites them into the life and light of the New Jerusalem, the Christian Church (22:1–5).

A CHRISTIAN MESSAGE IN AN APOCALYPTIC DRESS

As always in the teaching of the earliest Christian Church, John is aware that there will be a final coming of God at the end of all time (22:20). But his book focuses upon the victory already achieved in Jesus' death and resurrection.

In his letters to the seven churches of Asia, he reminds us that the Church as such is marked by ambiguity and sin (2:1–3:22). But he urges us to recognise what God has already done for us. He urges us to put our trust in his victory on the

INTRODUCTION

cross, so that we may be worthy members of what he describes as the New Jerusalem, the Church as it should be (21:1–22:5).

John of Patmos has made a remarkable contribution to Christian literature. He uses apocalyptic symbols and language, and unimaginable sequences of events, but he *bends the usual message of apocalyptic literature*. The language, symbols and narratives are apocalyptic, but the message is not. John does not point to what God will do for the evil and the good *in the future*. Rather, *he uses apocalyptic language and symbols to proclaim what God has done for us in and through the death and resurrection of Jesus. He claims that the effects of this victory have been available from the foundation of the world* (13:8). John asks that we respond accordingly. The message is about living the present in the light of God's victory in the death and resurrection of Jesus.

The Christian Reception of Revelation

Some early Christians doubted the value of Revelation, but the book was quickly accepted as a significant document. By the middle of the second century, Justin Martyr (100–165 CE) cited it as an authoritative Christian witness (*Dialogue with Trypho*, 80–81). Its eschatological interpretation became popular very early (e.g., Justin Martyr), but many disagreed, including "many good Christians" acknowledged by Justin Martyr (*Dialogue with Trypho*, 80.2), Origen (184–253 CE) and Eusebius of Caesarea (c. 260–340 CE). It was eventually included among the books of the Christian Bible in the definitive list of St Athanasius in 367 CE. Augustine's study of Revelation 20 (*City of God*, 20.7–17) in 426 CE led to the almost universal acceptance that John's document was about God's action to end time.

THE LAMB SLAIN FROM THE FOUNDATION OF THE WORLD (REV 13:8)

Most modern English translations of Rev 13:8, including the NRSV, translate Rev 13:8 as "whose name has not been written from the foundation of the world in the book of life of the Lamb that was slaughtered." Authors cannot accept that the event of Jesus' death (the slain Lamb) can be associated with the beginning of all time: "the Lamb that was slaughtered from the foundation of the world." But that is exactly what the Greek says! It is an important notion for John. Jesus died on a given day in history. But the effects of his death and resurrection touch God's creation from the beginnings to the end of all time.

INTRODUCTION

Above: Saint Augustine, icon by Tomas Giner, 1458, Spain (detail)

SAINT AUGUSTINE (354 – 430 CE)

St Augustine was a very influential figure from early Christian times. His writings have dominated Christian reflection on the doctrines of the Trinity, the person of Jesus Christ, the Sacraments, the interpretation of the Bible, sin and forgiveness, human frailty, what came to be known as the doctrine of Original Sin, and almost every other aspect of Christian life and thought. He was the first to devote detailed attention to Rev 20, especially vv. 2–6 which describe the "thousand-year reign" of Christ before Satan is freed for the final time. His interpretation does not situate this difficult passage within the broader message of Revelation. For Augustine, it is about God's final victory. Given his authority, the "end time" interpretation of John's work was widely adopted. The "new look" in Revelation studies questions his view.

THE "NEW LOOK" IN REVELATION STUDIES

Recent studies have made it clear that Emperor Domitian (81–96 CE) did not systematically persecute the Christian Church. John was not a prisoner at Patmos. Christians were not being persecuted for lack of attendance at the Emperor cults. Babylon may a symbol of unfaithful Jerusalem, not the city of Rome. The Roman Empire was not the primary focus of John's attention as the situation in Asia was calm and well governed. The "new look" in Revelation studies focuses more on the long-standing (and never-ending) conflict between good and evil. For John, Rome was its current manifestation. He was more concerned with God's victory over the perennial presence of evil, rather than just Rome.

INTRODUCTION

REVELATION AS A CHRISTIAN DOCUMENT

John has constructed his book upon a fourfold use of "sevens". Numbers play an important role in Revelation. The number "seven" indicates that a series is complete (not necessarily perfect: e.g., Rev 1:4, 20; 2:1–3:22; 5:6; 12:3), while the number "three" points to perfection (e.g., 1:4, 8; 4:8; 16:3; 22:13). Nowhere is this clearer than in the famous use of 666 as the number of the beast (13:18). The beast is condemned by its very name to a never-to-be-resolved frustration in its search for perfection. It is forever one number short of completion.

Another puzzling number is based upon the "seven weeks" of promised desolation that Israel must suffer, described in Daniel 9:24–27. John refers to "seven" years, or half of that, a broken time of three and a half years (see Dan 7:25; 12:7), or the same figure expressed as 42 months (Rev 11:2; 13:5), 1260 days (11:3), or "a time, two times, and half a time" (12:4) to indicate periods of suffering that will eventually lead to vindication. "Four" is associated with the earth and creation (4:6, 8; 5:6, 8, 9, 14; 17:15).

HARMAGEDON

This expression is found for the first time in Rev 16:16. It is regularly referred to in English as "the Armageddon" and associated with spectacular and violent epoch-making events. The tragic consequences of the COVID–19 virus across the whole world has been called "the Armageddon" of our era. Many contemporary movies portray a struggle to survive in a destroyed world as an Armageddon. Rendering the original Greek in English, as in the NRSV, produces Harmagedon, a combination of the Hebrew word for "mountain" (*har*) and the name of the city Meggido. Despite the popularity of the expression "Armageddon", we will use the biblical "Harmagedon".

Below: The SARS-CoV-2 virus causing COVID-19

Right: *Seven Golden Lampstands,* engraving after a drawing by Julius Schnorr von Carolsfeld

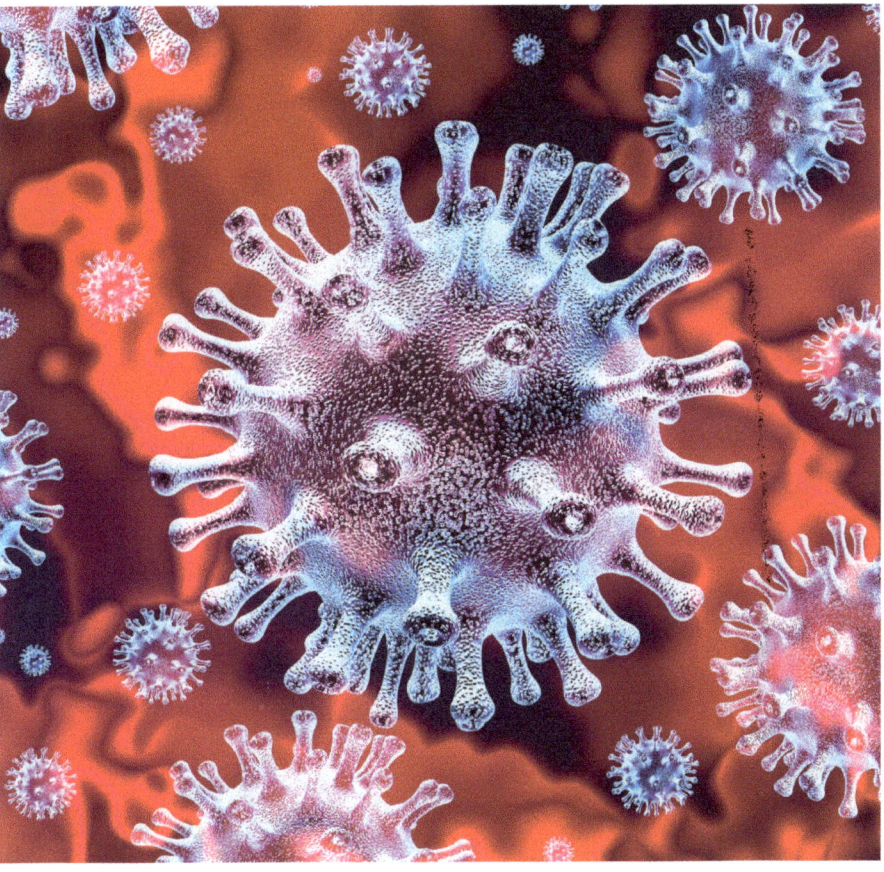

INTRODUCTION

KEY NOTES

◆ John makes use of the number "seven" at important moments in his narrative: letters, seals, trumpets and bowls.

◆ Each one of the "sevens" ends in a proclamation of the saving effects of Jesus' death and resurrection.

◆ The interpretations of the Book of Revelation have been the source of many acts of violence and tragedies across the centuries.

◆ The inclusion of the Book of Revelation as part of the Christian Bible suggests that we need to understand its message to Christians of all ages.

Why bother?

Revelation is not an easy book for a Christian of the third millennium to read and understand. What lies ahead promises to be "friendly", but there will be moments where the challenges of the use of apocalyptic language and symbols will make the reading of this *Friendly Guide* "difficult". Why bother? The abuse of this book from our Bible across the centuries asks us to make the effort.

Protestants and Catholics fired insults at one another in the sixteenth century by applying the image of the beast, and other nasty symbols, to one another. That practice continues among many Christian sects. The tragic siege at Waco, Texas (1993) was inspired by misdirected eschatological interpretation of the Book of Revelation and the Harmagedon. Some have interpreted the COVID–19 pandemic as a sign of God's justified anger in a wicked world.

One contemporary commentator has claimed: "Toxic poisons trickle from it. Consciousness-altering fumes waft out of it. Desperate hope and vindictive joy issue from it."[2]

There are good reasons for these claims, as the history of the interpretation of Revelation shows.[3] But they come from a faulty reading of a Christian book. What follows is a friendly guide through this challenging book. It uncovers a simple but profound message: The death and resurrection of Jesus was a victory over all evil. John invites us to enjoy the life and light now available in the New Jerusalem (22:1–5).

THE WACO SIEGE

Intolerance and cruel actions have long been inspired by reading Revelation as a prediction of the end time. The tragedy of Waco was a spectacular example. Led by David Koresh, the Branch Davidians were deeply committed to a literal reading of Revelation. Living in community at a location they named Mt Carmel, approximately 13 miles from the city of Waco, Texas, the group accepted Koresh's prophecy that the Harmagedon was about to happen. Uncertainty surrounds exactly who began the conflict. The USA taxation authorities investigating the settlement were fired upon. Four lives were lost. The FBI and the Texas Rangers joined the siege of Mt Carmel. It ran from 28 February until 19 April, 1993. Eighty-two Branch Davidians were killed, including David Koresh, and twenty-five children.

INTRODUCTION

SEARCHING FOR A ROAD MAP

Are there hints in the text of the Book of Revelation that John is "up to something"? Indeed there are. Can we use them to discern a "road map" that might guide us through the surprising twists and turns of this book?

We have already mentioned that, like many books, Revelation has a prologue and an epilogue.

They state and re-state the same message. Both announce that the book came from God through an angel to John, to show God's servants what takes place suddenly (1:1; 22:6, 16).

In both the prologue and the epilogue, John claims that his work is an authoritative interpretation of the Word of God, a prophecy (1:3; 22:7, 10, 18, 19). Both insist that those who attend to its message are blessed (1:3; 22:7). In both, God and Christ are called the Alpha and the Omega (1:8:22:13). Jesus Christ is described as the one who comes (1:7; 22:7, 12, 20). At the beginning and end of his book, John witnesses what he saw and heard (1:1–2, 4; 22:8). The audience is identified as those in the churches (1:4; 22:16). They respond "Yes" and "Amen" (1:7; 22:20).

John's fourfold use of "seven" leaps out even at a first reading of Revelation. There are letters to seven churches (2:1–3 :22), the opening of seven seals (6:1–8 :1), the blowing of seven trumpets (8:7–11:19) and seven bowls are poured out (16:1–21). Each of the "sevens" is prefaced by John's experiences of a heavenly encounter (1:9–20; 4:1–5:14; 8:2–6; 15: 1–8). What could be clearer? Enclosed within the "frame" of a prologue and an epilogue, the narrative is shaped by the use of "sevens".

PROLOGUES AND EPILOGUES

Among the Greeks, the action of a drama was prefaced by a prologue, providing the essential message of the story, and an epilogue, which closed the event. This literary practice is found in the Gospels. The prologue of John 1:1–18 is matched by the Gospel's conclusion in 20:30–31. The prologue of Mark 1:1–13 is matched by the epilogue of 16:1–8. Matthew's Gospel promises that the son to be born will be named "'Emmanuel', which means 'God is with us'" (Matt 1:23). The final words in the Gospel are Jesus' promise: "I am with you always" (28:20). John's direct appeal to his audience in Rev 1:1–8 and 22:6–21 is a further example of this traditional practice.

INTRODUCTION

SEVENS

Unfortunately, things are not so simple. The first half of the Book of Revelation can be shaped by following the "sevens".

Prologue (1:1–8)
a. A heavenly encounter that commissions John to write what the one like the Son of Man says to the churches (1:9–20), and the letters to the *seven churches* (3:1–22).
b. A heavenly encounter that commissions the slain but standing Lamb as worthy to open the seals (4:1–5:14), and the opening of the *seven seals* in a sequence of 4 + 3 (6:1–8:1).
c. A heavenly encounter that commissions seven angels with trumpets (8:2–6), and the blowing of the *seven trumpets* in a sequence of 4 + 3 (8:7–11:19).

But the end of chapter 11 is where this regular narrative rhythm of a heavenly encounter followed by one of the "sevens" disappears. It will not return until 15:1–16:21.

What does the interpreter make of 12:1–14:20 and 17:1–22:5? Making sense of both sections where the narrative pattern appears to be broken depends on our understanding of the pouring out of the seven bowls. The description of the Harmagedon of 16:1–21 is a symbolic presentation of the victory of Christ's death and resurrection over all evil forces.

What follows in 17:1–22:5 can be understood as a description of the destruction that will come with the establishment of God and his Christ in the New Jerusalem. But the sequence of the woman clothed with the sun (12:1–18), the appearance of the two beasts (13:1–18), the Lamb with the 144,000, and the one like the Son of Man accompanied by six angels (14:1–20) generates difficulty.

Above: *Frogs from dragon's mouth* from Apocalypse of Saint-Sever, Paris, 11th cent

ALL EVIL POWERS ARE DESTROYED

And I saw three foul spirits like frogs coming from the mouth of the dragon. These are the demonic spirits, performing signs, who go abroad to the kings of the whole world, to assemble them for battle on the great day of God the Almighty. … And they assembled them at the place that in Hebrew is called Harmagedon. The seventh angel poured his bowl into the air, and a loud voice came out of the temple, from the throne, saying, "It is done!" (Rev 16:15–16, 18).

"Most attempts to discover the structure of Revelation have found it particularly difficult to see how chapters 12–14 fit into the overall structure."[4]

The whole of 12:1–22:5 depends upon the pouring out of the bowls in a pattern of 4 + 3, preceded by its heavenly encounter, in 15:1–16:21. The Harmagadon (16:16) is the centrepiece of the second half of John's narrative. Our road map directs us through three episodes that *prepare* for 16:1–21, and three further episodes spell out the *consequences* of 16:1–21 (see page 7 for a simple outline of this literary structure).

d. The threefold *preparation* for the pouring out of the bowls (12:1–18: the woman, the son, and the serpent; 13:1–18: the two beasts; 14: 1–20: the salvation of the faithful in Israel).
e. A heavenly encounter that commissions seven angels with seven bowls (15:1–8), and the pouring out of the seven bowls in a sequence of 4 + 3: God's victory in and through Christ at the Harmagadon of the cross (16:1–21).
f. The threefold *consequences* of the death of Christ (17:1–19:10: the vision of the destruction of Babylon; 19:11–21:8: the vision of the destruction of all evil powers; 21:9–22:5: the vision of the heavenly Jerusalem and the gathering of the faithful).

Epilogue (22:6–21).

INTRODUCTION

Above: St John receiving the Book of Revelation; mosaic in Patmos, Greece

"SUDDENLY" OR "SOON"

Different forms of the Greek word *tachus* appear regularly across Revelation (1:1; 2:16; 3:11; 11:14; 22:6, 7, 12, 20). It can mean either in a short time ("soon") or the speed of an action ("quickly"). The dominant "end-time" reading of Revelation claims that John is forecasting an imminent end of history ("soon"). We suggest that it teaches that the saving effects of Jesus' death and resurrection happen "quickly". Revelation is not communicating when God will act ("soon"), but how ("quickly"). In what follows, where the NRSV indicates "soon", I will offer my own translation of the Greek as "suddenly" or "quickly".

KEY NOTES

◆ Many books, both ancient and modern, begin with a prologue, and return to the message of the prologue in an epilogue.

◆ Most interpreters accept that John is telling the churches that the events he will describe will happen "soon", but he is in fact writing about something that happens "quickly."

◆ The book is either about the imminent end time (soon), or the saving inbreak of God in the events of Jesus' death and resurrection (quickly).

◆ If John, writing about 96 CE, expected God's final intervention "soon" – he was wrong.

◆ The problem of the design of Revelation is eased by recognising that everything depends upon the "sevens", with the pouring out of the seven bowls (16:1–21), involving a *preparation* (12:1–14:20) and its *consequences* (17:1–22:5).

THE PROLOGUE AND THE LETTERS
REVELATION 1:1—3:22

THE PROLOGUE: 1:1–8

John's dense first page sets the program for his book: what God had done for us in Jesus Christ. However, this revelation takes place across two "eras". The first is a revelation that comes to John through the mediation of an angel who passed it on to John (v. 1). It is an authoritative teaching (a "prophecy") of the word of God and a witness to the coming of Jesus Christ. Angels have long been mediators between God and God's people. This "era" tells of the revelation of the saving presence of God throughout Israel's history; those who read and hear it are blessed (vv. 2–3).

John then addresses his audience, the seven churches (v. 4). Here we meet the number "seven" for the first time: the seven churches represent "the Church". They receive the revelation that belongs to the "era" that follows the death and resurrection of Jesus Christ. They are greeted with grace and peace that comes from God, described in a threefold form: the one who is (God), the one who is coming (Jesus Christ), and the seven spirits before the throne of God (v. 4). We meet the perfect number "three" for the first time. The coming of Christ and the shedding of his blood have generated a priestly people who serve God, to whom all glory is due (vv. 5–6). Using imagery from Daniel 7:13 and Zechariah 12:10–14, John presents Jesus as a messianic figure who must suffer, bringing judgment upon humankind (v. 7). The whole of history is in view, from the time of Israel until the time of the Church. God is the Alpha and the Omega, the Lord of that history (v. 8).

THE ONE WHO IS COMING
The NRSV and most translations of Rev 1:4 refer to Jesus Christ as "who is to come". However, the Greek word *(ho erchomenos)* is in the present tense. John wishes to tell his audience that he "is coming". It refers to the death and resurrection of Jesus, whose effects are among us, not to some future return of Jesus as judge.

THE SEVEN LETTERS: 1:9–3:22

Heavenly encounter: 1:9–20

The heavenly encounter of 1:9–20 situates the Christian missionary John on the island of Patmos (v. 9). In the Spirit on the Lord's day, he initially "heard a loud voice behind me like a trumpet" (v. 10). Trumpets have long been associated with communication between God and humankind during the time of Israel, especially in the gift of the Law on Sinai (see Exod 19:16–19; 20:18. See also Heb 12:19). The voice "from behind" instructs John that he must write to the seven churches (v. 11). At this stage the fullness of the message is hidden, the beginnings of the revelation of Jesus Christ in Israel's history.

The hiddenness is overcome as John turns and sees the heavenly counterpart of the Jerusalem temple and its liturgy: seven golden lampstands. The one like the Son of Man stands in their midst. Jesus Christ is at the heart of the heavenly Jerusalem. John regularly uses the colours gold and white to symbolise a heavenly reality. The lampstands are golden, and the one like the Son of Man wears a golden sash (vv. 12–13). The description of the one like the Son of Man, taken largely from Daniel and Ezekiel, follows. He is a powerful, heavenly authority, holding the seven stars. They are seven heavenly counterparts of the churches (v. 20). Only he can exercise the sword of judgment, so authoritative is his presence (vv. 14–16). John collapses "as though dead." He is raised by the right hand of the one like the Son of Man (v. 17).

The raising of John is a symbol of the one like the Son of Man, the first and the last. He was dead but is alive. He has power over death and Hades, the dwelling place of the dead. The death and resurrection of Jesus has transformed history. The Book of Revelation will tell how that transformation took place in God's victory over evil. The one like the Son of Man commands John to write what he has seen to this point. He must tell the remarkable sequence of events that follow in rapid succession across the rest of the book: "what is to take place after this" (v. 19). John writes what the one like the Son of Man commands him to write to the seven churches (2:1, 8, 12, 18, 3:1, 7, 14).

THE IDEA OF A HEAVENLY COUNTERPART

Every imperfect human creation was thought to have a perfect heavenly counterpart in heaven. A true Israel exists in heaven, as does every true Israelite. The temple also had its imperfections, but a true and spotless temple existed in heaven. The Jewish and Christian idea of a "guardian angel" derives from this belief.

Far left: The angels standing guard to the seven churches of Asia, anonymous
Left: Mosaic from Patmos

THE SEVEN CHURCHES

Although we have reports of Paul's presence in Ephesus (see Acts 18–20), we know very little of the churches in Smyrna, Pergamum, Thyatira, Sardis, Philadelphia, and Laodicea. Each of the letters is structured in the same fashion:

- **Address**
- **Presentation of Christ as the one who sends the letter**
- **Praise, correction, warning, advice to the churches**
- **Announcement of Christ's coming**
- **Invitation to listen to the voice of the Spirit**
- **Promises to the victor.**

Even though some churches seem to be better than others, the same corrections and warnings are found across all seven: lax living, preparedness to accept a pagan way of life and practice, "fornication", language used by Israel's prophets (especially Isaiah, Jeremiah, and Ezekiel) to refer to the adoration of false Gods. Perhaps they were accommodating the cult of the Roman Emperor too easily. Asian Christians were experiencing local tensions with Jewish communities. All seven churches were experiencing the same problems, some more than others. Living as committed Christians amid the glamour of the Greco-Roman world was a challenge. But into the compliments and the warnings of these letters, John insinuates God's sacred history in Israel.

Christians at *Ephesus* (Rev 2:1–7) have performed well. But they have abandoned the love they had at first (v. 4). This is an allusion to the original fall of humankind reported in Genesis 3. The promise made to the victorious at Ephesus confirms this: "I will give permission to eat from the tree of life that is in the paradise of God" (v. 7. See Gen 2:15–17; 3:1–7). Christians at *Smyrna* (Rev 2:8–11) have been abandoned by Judaism, its religious parent. But allusion to the "ten days" of affliction looks back to the ten plagues of Israel's presence in Egypt (Rev 2:10. See Exod 7–11). As in Egypt, they are afflicted, suffer poverty, and are imprisoned (vv. 9–10. See Exod 1:8–14; 2:23–25). The victorious will be given "the crown of life" (Rev 2:10), and they will not be harmed by the "second death." As in Egypt, perseverance brings life-giving rewards.

The situation of the church in *Pergamum* refers to characters and experiences of Israel's exodus from Egypt (vv. 12–17). In the first place, they run the danger of "fornication", adoring false Gods in their longing to return to Egypt (Exod 16:2–3; 17:3, etc.) and their worship of the golden calf (Exod 32–34). The influence of the prophet Balaam over King Balak is recalled (Rev 2:14. See Num 22:1–25:25; 31:16). In Rev 2:17 the victors are promised "hidden manna" (Exod 16:13–36) and a white stone, recalling the stones on the shoulders of the Ephod, a special sleeveless garment worn by the high priest (Exod 28:9–14). The stones carried the names of the children of Israel.

Allusions to the time of Israel's kings dominate the letter to *Thyatira* (Rev 2:18–29.): increasing wealth, power, and expansion (v. 19) that led to material and spiritual corruption. The name "Jezebel" captures this. She was the foreign and cruel wife of Ahab (1 Kings 16:31).

She instigated the murder of Naboth (21:1–14). Elijah's prophecy against Ahab, his wife, her lovers and her children (21:17–24) matches the threats issued to Christians in Thyatira (Rev 2:22–23). The instructions to *Sardis* (3:1–6) warn against mediocrity. They recall the state of desolation and death that followed the destruction of the kingdoms of Israel and Judah. God's chosen people were as if dead, reduced to a "remnant" of faithful (v. 2. See Isa 65:8–10; Ezek 37:1–14). The remnant is represented by "the few persons" who are worthy (Rev 3:4).

Facing the allure of the Greco-Roman world, the Christians at *Philadelphia* (3:7–13) are instructed by steady allusions to a building: keys (v. 7), construction (v. 8), door (v. 8), a column in the temple (v. 12), city of God (v. 12), the new Jerusalem (v. 12) and the "name" of God and of Jesus that will be written on the pillar in the temple (v. 12). The community has "little power" (v. 8). After the return from the exile in Babylon (539 CE), a struggling and impoverished community attempted to re-establish itself and rebuild a sanctuary. The biblical record has come to the threshold of the time of Jesus Christ.

Finally, there is no praise for the sinful church at *Laodicea* (3:14–22). Its failures are relentlessly condemned (vv. 14–17). The call to repentance in vv. 18–20 is striking. They are to adorn themselves with gold and white and return to true sight (v. 18). The harsh words of the one like the Son of Man have been spoken out of love (v. 19). Because of that, they are promised participation at the messianic meal: "I am standing at the door knocking; if you hear my voice and open the door, I will come in to you and eat with you, and you with me" (v. 20).

The letters address problems in the Church as a whole, tempted in so many ways by surrounding pagan society. But they are also a guided reading through the key moments of the Hebrew Scriptures, an essential part of the "revelation of Jesus Christ" (1:1). The words to the victors at the end of each letter promise participation in God's messianic kingdom (2:7, 11, 17, 26–28; 3:5–6, 12; 21). Israel's sacred history, from the creation story (Ephesus) to the promise of a place at the table of the messianic banquet (Laodicea), has made God's design known. This is the message of the rest of the Book of Revelation: Jesus Christ's death and resurrection give meaning to the whole of Scripture.

Far left: Map of the seven churches of Revelation (Asia Minor)

Below: Seven churches of Asia in the east window at York Minster

KEY NOTES

◆ John's opening message in the Book of Revelation is to praise God because Jesus Christ has saved believers and founded a priestly people.

◆ The Book of Revelation insists upon two "eras" in the revelation of God's saving action in Jesus: from creation until the death and resurrection of Jesus, and from the foundation of the Church until the end of time.

◆ These two eras are represented by John's *hearing* a voice from behind, and then his turning to *see* the golden lampstands and the one like the Son of Man.

◆ The seven letters are directed to the Church itself, although current problems in the Asian churches are also raised.

◆ The backdrop to the seven letters is a summary of Israel's sacred history, from creation to the promise of participation in the messianic banquet.

Left: *The Light of the World* by Holman Hunt

Right: *Receiving the White Robes* from Douce Apocalypse, Bodleian MS 180

THE OPENING OF THE SEVEN SEALS
REVELATION 4:1–8:1

In the vision that prefaces the opening of the seven seals, John sees God, Lord of all creation (4:1–11), and the slain yet living Lamb (5:1–14).

THE HEAVENLY ENCOUNTER: 4:1–5:14

GOD AND CREATION (4:1–11)

The voice like a trumpet that announced God's revelation in Israel's story (1:10) invites John through an open door (4:1) into the heavenly sphere. John is again "in the spirit" (1:10) as he has a vision of God (vv. 2–3). A heavenly company sings God's praise (vv. 4–8). God is holy (v. 8) and worthy of glory and honour "for you created all things, and by your will they existed and were created" (v. 11).

The one on the throne is a divine figure, brilliant in appearance and encircled by a rainbow (vv. 2–3). The flashes of lightning, rumblings and peals of thunder that come from the throne add to the description of the indescribable. A heavenly court surrounds him. Twenty-four elders are also seated upon thrones, dressed in white, and wear golden crowns. They belong to the heavenly, are close to the one on the throne, but are lesser figures (v. 4). The seven flaming torches in front of the throne are "the seven spirits of God", the fullness of the spirit whose presence in heaven recalls the creative activity of the Spirit of God moving across the crystal clear waters of God's creation (vv. 5–6a. See Gen 1:1–2).

The four living creatures (vv. 6–7) are associated with the earth: the four elements, the four winds, the four corners of the earth. Their description comes from the four-faced angels in Ezekiel 1:6. But John's four living creatures each have a single face: like a lion, like an ox, like a human being, like an eagle. Each living creature will soon play a role in opening the first four seals (6:1, 3, 5, 7). With their all-seeing eyes, they govern the earth (v. 8a). They unceasingly praise God, the Almighty, the one who is and who is coming.

This description of the heavenly court in 4:1–11 summarises Israel's faith in God as the creator of all things. The threefold acclamation of God's holiness, however, points to another era. Most translations, including the NRSV, state that "whenever" the living creatures sing God's praise, the twenty-four elders prostrate themselves and praise the creator (vv. 9–11). The Greek text says that "when" (Greek: *hotan*) glory is given to God, the twenty four elders will give (Greek: *dōsousin*), glory and honour, will fall down (Greek: *pesousin*), will worship (Greek: *proskunēsousin*), and will cast down (Greek: *balousin*) their crowns. The response of the twenty-four elders is yet to take place. The presentation of Israel's faith in God as the creator of all things awaits fulfilment.

That occasion is at hand. On the appearance of the Lamb, joined by many angels, the twenty-four elders prostrate themselves and worship (5:8, 14). All honour and praise will be given to the creator God (4:11) after the slain and risen Lamb has taken the scroll from God's right hand. Only then is the subordination of all powers and authorities to the creator God and the redeeming Lamb is complete (5:8b–14).

The Lamb and universal salvation (5:1–14)

Revelation 4:1–11 and 5:1–14 form a continuous narrative. The one seated on the throne holds a scroll written on back and front in his right hand. It is locked by seven seals (5:1). A mighty angel asks if there is anyone "worthy" of opening the seven seals, but no one "in heaven or in earth" is worthy (vv. 2–3). A problem exists in heaven! John begins to weep, but is told to desist. Israel's Messiah, the Lion of the Tribe of Judah, the Root of David is worthy to open the seals because he "has conquered" (vv. 4–5).

A dramatic presentation of Israel's Messiah follows. In a location of intense familiarity with God (between the one on the throne and the twenty-four elders), John sees "a Lamb standing as if it had been slaughtered". John has been told that Israel's Messiah "has conquered" (v. 5). He is told how: through the death and resurrection of Jesus Christ. The Messiah is all powerful (seven horns) and sees all things (seven eyes), and the fullness of the Spirit (seven spirits of God) proceeds from him to all the earth (v. 6). He receives the scroll from the right hand of the one on the throne (v. 7).

The heavenly court's acclamation of God and the Lamb follows. Holding harps and golden bowls of incense, signs of the prayers of all the "saints" who have kept the

THE LAMB RECEIVED THE SCROLL

Many translations, including the NRSV, say that the Lamb "took" the scroll in 5:7 and 8. The Greek verb (*lambanō*) can mean "to take", but it also means "to receive". For John, and all early Christian thinking about Jesus, he "receives" his mission from God. This is what is meant in Rev 5:7 when John writes that the Lamb received the scroll "from the right hand of the one who is seated on the throne".

Above: *The Lamb of God* by Francisco de Zurbaran
Far left: Tile mosaic of Jesus Christ in the Exeter Cathedral, Exeter, England

KEY NOTES

◆ The narrative of Rev 4:1–5:14 is often compared to a sacred liturgy.

◆ Israel's Scriptures acclaim that God is the creator of all things.

◆ Christian tradition continues that acclamation, adding that the death and resurrection of Jesus Christ have given the possibility of divine life to all creation.

word of God and believed in the promises of the prophets, the court "fell down" (Greek: *epesan*). They affirm the worthiness of the Lamb to open the seven seals of the book that contains a long history of evil from which humankind must be set free. Only the Lamb is worthy to unseal it because he was slaughtered, and his blood has ransomed all people for God, making them into a kingdom of priests serving God. Those saved from evil by the death and resurrection of Jesus Christ will overcome evil powers and reign on earth. The saving victory of Jesus' death and resurrection is proclaimed (vv. 8–10). Myriads and myriads of angels surrounding the throne join with the four living creatures and the twenty-four elders. They sing the praise of the Lamb. His death and resurrection bring due power, wealth, wisdom, might, honour, glory, and blessing.

Heavenly characters praise the Lamb (vv. 11–12). The whole universe joins the song. Every creature in heaven, on the earth, and under the earth sings praise. They honour both the one seated on the throne (4:2-3) and the Lamb (5:6, 13). Only now, with God and the Lamb honoured and praised, is the expected obeisance of the four living creatures completed: "And the elders fell down (Greek: *epesan*) and worshipped" (Greek: *prosekunēsan*) (vv. 13–14). What was promised in the future tenses of 4:9–11 takes place for the first time in 5:14 (see also 7:11).

THE SAINTS

John often refers to "the saints", frequently associating them with those who lived by the Word of God and the witness to Christ. Often interpreted as Christian martyrs, they are the "holy ones of Israel" who lived by the Law and accepted the messianic witness of the Prophets. They are the "saints" from the history of Israel (see Dan 7:19-21).

There is only one revelation of Jesus Christ, but it takes place across two stages. It begins in the recognition of God as the Lord and Creator proclaimed by Israel's Scriptures (4:1–11). The death and resurrection of Jesus broach a new era. The saving effects of the blood of the Lamb make possible the long-awaited universal availability of divine life (5:1–14). Now both the God of Israel and Jesus Christ, the Lamb, are praised and honoured. The Lamb opens all seven seals (6:1, 3, 5, 7, 9, 12; 8:1). As the Lamb opens the first four seals, one of the four living creatures (4:6–7) calls forth the four horses and their riders (6:1, 3, 5, 7).

THE OPENING OF THE SEVEN SEALS: 6:1–8:1

KEY NOTES

◆ The message behind the opening of the first four seals adopts themes from the Book of Genesis.

◆ The opening of the first seal announces humankind's potential for good, as in God's original creative design.

◆ The opening of the other three seals, alluding to Genesis, show what happens when evil predominates: war, hunger, suffering and death.

The opening of the first four seals (6:1–8)

The first horse to appear is white. The audience knows that white is associated with the divine. The rider is adorned with a bow and a crown, further signs that the presentation of the white horse anticipates a good result. "He came out conquering and to conquer" (v. 2). The white horse and its rider represent the rich possibilities of humankind. But the bow can be a weapon of destruction (see Isa 41:2) or a means to become a great nation, as in God's gift of a bow to Hagar (see Gen 21:17–21). A choice must be made. Ultimate trust must be in the Lord, not in the bow or the sword (Ps 44:6). Men and women have the *potential* to make the right choice. The remaining horses and their riders show the result of decisions for evil.

Right: *Four Riders of the Apocalypse* **from the Book of Revelation**

Dürer presents all four horsemen as bringing destruction. This is not the case for the first horseman who wears white and comes to conquer with his God-given bow.

The second horse is bright red, a colour associated with war and violence (v. 3). The rider is given a great sword. He is "permitted to take peace from the earth" (v. 4). Suffering and warfare result from humankind's choice of evil, as the audience knows from the first account of a murder in the story of Cain and Abel (Gen 4:1–12).

The third horse is black. The rider holds a measuring scale (v. 5). A voice from the four living creatures announces a lack of essential foods: bread, wine, and oil. The Genesis story explains how the fall from innocence led to the universal struggle to produce and provide sufficient food: "By the sweat of your face you shall eat bread" (Gen 3:19).

The fourth horse is pallid green, the colour of a dead body (vv. 7–8a). Sin produces death (Gen 3:2–6). The fall into sinfulness leads to death and to the dwelling place of the dead, Hades.

John concludes his presentation of the opening of the first four seals with a summary of the consequences of humankind's loss of innocence (first seal): death by

KEY NOTES

◆ All the signs that accompany "the wrath of the Lamb" come from the biblical tradition of events that will mark the end of time.

◆ In the Book of Revelation this meaning is changed, as they are now applied to the judgment than flows from the death and resurrection of the Lamb.

◆ History does not end with these signs but belongs to the holy ones from Israel's history and to a countless multitude of Christian believers who are cared for and nourished by God and the Lamb.

Left: *Death on the Pale Horse* **by Gustave Dore**

> ### KEY NOTES
>
> ◆ The Gospels of Mark (15:33), Matthew (27:45) and Luke (Luke 23:44–45) report that the death of Jesus was marked by a period of silence.
>
> ◆ This "silence" is highlighted in the Christian celebration of Holy Saturday, in the silence between Good Friday and Easter Sunday.
>
> ◆ Tradition has linked this period of silence "on earth" with a time when the crucified Christ descends into the depths, bringing salvation to the whole of creation, from the beginning of time.

sword (second seal), pestilence (third seal), and wild animals (fourth seal). But only one-fourth of the earth is destroyed (Rev 6:8b). There is still hope.

The opening of the fifth seal (6:9–11)

The first signs of hope appear in John's sight "under the altar of those who had been slaughtered for the word of God and for the testimony they had given" (v. 9). Who are these people? Continuing his development of God's sacred history, John describes those from Israel's history who, in the midst of the violence that comes from sin, have adhered to the word of God and have lived in the hope of the messianic witness of the Prophets. They are the same people as "the saints" of 5:8. They have been "given a white robe" (v. 11) and thus already participate in the divine life. However, they do not mark the end point of God's design.

They belong to the history of Israel and are waiting for the final event that will make sense of that past. They ask how long they must wait (v. 10). They must "rest a little longer" (11). The death and resurrection of Jesus will mark the beginnings of a new era. John's vision informs his audience that there is a time *before* Jesus' death when the saints in Israel were given a white robe. As we will see as the sixth seal is, there is a time *after* that event when believers from every nation, tribe, people and tongue are "robed in white" (7:9). For the moment, the saints of Israel must rest until their number is complete (6:11).

The opening of the sixth seal (6:12–7:17)

The opening of the sixth seal (6:12–7:17), the blowing of the sixth trumpet (9:12–10:14), and the pouring out of the seventh bowl (16:12–16) are richly developed. They each announce the saving effects of the death and resurrection of Jesus.

As the Lamb opens the sixth seal, a series of traditionally accepted apocalyptic signs bursts into the narrative. The "wrath of the Lamb" (6:16) judges all evil but is not the end of the world. End-time imagery is used: a great earthquake, the blackening of the sun, the falling of the stars of the sky, the rolling up of the sky like a scroll, the shaking of the mountains, the humiliation of all, hiding in the caves and rocks of the mountains (vv. 12–16). As the Lamb executes a judgment symbolised by these traditional end-time horrors, now drawn into history to describe God's perennial conflict with evil, the question is asked: "Who is able to stand?" (v. 17).

It is immediately answered. The four angels that rule the earth (4:6–7), who have called forth the riders and the horses as the first four seals were opened, are instructed by another angel. This angel is commissioned by God. Everything must be put on hold so that "the servants of our God" can be marked with a divine seal.

Above: *The Harrowing of Hell* by Fra Angelico

A widespread iconic tradition in Eastern Christianity portrays the crucified
but victorious Jesus' descent into the depths of the earth.
He takes Adam and Eve by the hand,
raising them up to heaven as kings and prophets look on.
The icons are associated with Holy Saturday,
but they can also be interpreted as representing
the timeless and perennial effects of the death and resurrection of Jesus.
His death and resurrection have brought
life and salvation "from the foundation of the world" (Rev 13:8).

These are the ones who stand tall before the wrath of the Lamb (6:17).

They are formed by two groups. The first is a gathering of one hundred and forty-four thousand, twelve thousand from each of the tribes that formed Israel's history (vv. 4–8). The second is a universal gathering, "a great multitude that no one could count, from every nation, from all tribes and peoples and languages". They are standing before the throne and the Lamb. They carry the palm of victory and are robed in white (v. 9). They populate the two eras of God's saving presence: Israel's sacred history that culminated in the death and the resurrection of Jesus (vv. 4–8), and people that cannot be numbered or classified by race or tribe (v. 9).

In 4:9–11 John points out that the heavenly court will eventually fall and worship. It begins in 5:13–14. In 7:11, the angels, the elders and the four living creatures again fall (Greek: *epesan*) before the throne and worship (Greek: *prosekunēsan*) God (v. 12).

But one of the elders asks John where the great multitude with palms and robed in white come from (v. 13). John turns the question back on the elder (v. 14). He reveals that they come from the great ordeal. "They have washed their robes and made them white in the blood of the Lamb" (v. 14). They enjoy participation in the divine life because of the death and resurrection of Jesus who has "freed us from our sins with his blood" (1:5b).

This revelation leads the elder to a hymn praising God and the Lamb. The universal salvific effects of the death and resurrection of Jesus recounted across the opening of the sixth seal generate praise of God who will protect the faithful (vv. 15–16) and the Lamb who will be their shepherd and comforter (v. 17).

The opening of the seventh seal (8:1)

The opening of the seventh seal produces approximately a half hour of silence in heaven. The silence of heaven matches the Gospel accounts of the silence that accompanied the death of Jesus (Mark 15:33; Matt 27:45; Luke 23:44–45). The ancient Christian theme of Jesus' descent into the depths begins here (see also 1 Peter 3:17–20). Written much later (fourth or fifth century), an anonymous Christian preacher catches the meaning of 8:1:

> There is great silence on earth today, and great silence and stillness. The whole earth keeps silence because the King is asleep. The earth trembled and is still because God has fallen asleep in the flesh and he has raised up all who have slept ever since the world began (*An Ancient Homily for Holy Saturday*).

The saving effects of the death and resurrection of Jesus have given life to all the saints "before the foundation of the world" (Rev 13:8).

THE BLOWING OF THE SEVEN TRUMPETS
REVELATION 8:2–11:19

THE HEAVENLY ENCOUNTER: 8:2–6

John sees members of the angelic host ("seven angels") who are given seven trumpets. The first part of his vision is the heavenly model of Israel's cult: a golden altar and a further angel with a golden censer. The incense of the heavenly liturgy raises the prayers of the saints of Israel to God (vv. 2–4). Dramatically, the angel fills the censer with fire and casts it down, accompanied by "peals of thunder, rumblings, flashes of lightning, and earthquakes" (v. 5). The period of the saints of Israel comes to an end, as another era begins. In the Gospels, fire and earth-shaking events accompanied the death and resurrection of Jesus (Mark 15:33–39; Matt 27:45–54; 28:1–4; Luke 23:44–45). In the Gospel of Luke, Jesus announces, "I have come to bring fire to the earth, and how I wish it were already kindled!" (Luke 12:49). The death and resurrection of Jesus will bring a judging fire. This is the "fire from the altar" thrown down upon the earth (Rev 8:5). The heavenly encounter closes as the angels who have the seven trumpets make ready to blow them (v. 6).

KEY NOTES

◆ John uses images from the Jewish Scriptures and other literature that point to the end of time.

◆ He draws them back into human history to describe the perennial presence of evil in the world and society.

◆ By using imagery from the Book of Exodus, there is always a hint of a positive outcome.

Above: *The Third Trumpet*, from the Douce Apocalypse, Bodleian MS 180

Far right: *Seven Trumpets* from Welles Apocalypse

THE BLOWING OF THE SEVEN TRUMPETS: 8:7–11:19

THE BLOWING OF THE FIRST FOUR TRUMPETS (8:7–13)

Looking back at the destruction that led to Israel's exodus from Egypt, hail and fire, mixed with blood, fall upon the earth at the blowing of the first trumpet (8:7). The hurling down of heavenly fire burns up a third of the trees and the green grass (see Exod 9:22–35). But only a third is destroyed. Not everything is lost.

At the blowing of the second trumpet, a fiery mountain is thrown down into the sea (Rev 8:8–9). As in the second plague in Egypt, the waters turn into blood (Exod 7:17–25). A third of the living creatures die, and a third of the commercial life on the sea is destroyed.

The blowing of the third trumpet causes a great star to be thrown down into a third of the rivers and springs (Rev 8:10–11). The star makes the waters bitter. Many die from the bitterness. The bitter waters of Marah are recalled (see Exod 15:22–25), but there is still hope, as there was during the Exodus.

Nothing is thrown down at the blowing of the fourth trumpet (Rev 8:12–13). All the illumination of the world is struck and lose a third of their light. They no longer perform the task for which they were created by God.

The trumpets tell of falling angels from heaven, damaging the whole of God's creation. Sin and evil are rampant. Although human beings necessarily suffer (v. 11), the focus is upon a damaged creation. Only one-third of the creation is destroyed. Hints of a future liberation from evil exists in the repeated allusions to the themes from Israel's exodus. God's presence in failure led to freedom.

Closing his report of the blowing of the first four trumpets, John tells of "an eagle with a loud voice" in mid-heaven (v. 13). The association of an eagle with the exodus (see Exod 19:4; Deut 32:11) continues to promise hope in punishment. The blowing of the final three trumpets leads to three "woes" that sin and evil will bring upon the inhabitants of the earth. Israel's ambiguous history was not an end-in-itself. It promised a future liberation.

THE BLOWING OF THE FIFTH TRUMPET, THE FIRST "WOE" (9:1–12)

The falling star of the third trumpet (7:10) is identified as Satan, who had fallen from heaven to earth and had been given the key to the bottomless pit (9:1). This refers to a primeval time, before Jesus Christ who alone now holds the keys of death and Hades (1:17b–18). Satan may dwell in the bottomless pit, whose horrors are described (9:2), but he has authority to send out his agents: locust-like scorpions (vv. 3–12). The plague of locusts from the Exodus is recalled (Exod 10:3–20), but they act differently. They do not damage the vegetation (v. 4a); they inflict torture like scorpions (Rev 9:5). The pain is so severe that those inflicted wish to lose themselves. Caught in evil, they remain locked in their rejection of God, unable to escape (v. 6). "Only those people who do not have the seal of God on their foreheads" (v. 4b) are tortured. Those from Israel and the countless other multitudes who have "washed their robes ... in the blood of the Lamb" (7:9–17) do not experience the frustrated suffering that results from sin and evil.

The rest of the first "woe" is a description of the locusts (vv. 7–10) and the naming of their king (v. 11). They are powerful but have no authority; they wear false crowns (v. 7). They are horrifyingly human-looking, ready for war, generating a sound like many chariots (vv. 8–9), inflicting pain for five months (v. 10). Their time is limited. The name of their king is the name of the place where Satan rules among the wicked (see Prov 15:11; Ps 88:11; Job 26:6). For the moment, Satan rules over death and Hades (v. 11). But that will not always be the case.

The blowing of the sixth trumpet, the second "woe" (9:13–11:14)

As with the opening of the sixth seal (6:12–7:17), the blowing of the sixth trumpet is more extensive. It has three distinct moments: warfare as the severest consequence of the fall of humankind (9:13–21), God's initial intervention in Israel's sacred history (10:1–11) and God's presence in Israel through the temple, the Law, and the prophets (11:1–14).

KEY NOTES

◆ John persists in his use of end-time symbols to refer to the historical effects of evil.

◆ In the first and second "woe" he uses these symbols to focus upon the evil effects of death through warfare.

◆ Even in the tragic description of warfare, John hints that God can respond to this evil.

KEY NOTES

- A scroll is used in Israel to symbolise the Sacred Scriptures.

- John presents the Sacred Scriptures of Israel as God's presence among his people.

- John uses the "small" scroll that leaves a bitter taste once consumed as a symbol of Scriptures that are not God's final word.

- The Jerusalem temple was a visible sign of God's presence and care in Israel.

- The presence of the Law and the prophets provided the people of God access to the ways of God in the world.

- In Matthew 23:37 and Luke 13:24 Jesus accused Jerusalem of slaying the prophets.

Below: Wailing Wall, as it is today

Right: St John holding the Book, Patmos

A voice from the heavenly altar commands the trumpet-blowing angel to release "the four angels who are bound at the great river Euphrates" (9:13–14). Held back earlier so that they could do no damage (7:1), they are set loose "to kill a third of humankind" (v. 15). The Euphrates was regarded as the birthplace of worldly empires. The "winds" of Daniel 7 stirred the waters that set free the four beasts that brought war and disaster upon Israel (Dan 7:4–8). The four angels are set free to unleash a huge army.

The number of the cavalry troops is extraordinary: two hundred million (v. 16). The horses are demonic, dressed for war. They wear armour and breathe smoke with the colours of fire, sapphire, and sulphur (vv. 17–18). A third of humankind is slain (v. 18). With their mouths and their serpent-like tails, the horses inflict harm (v. 19). This suffering and death does not produce repentance among those who are not slain by the plagues of war. They continue to worship false idols. They cannot desist from the murder, sorcery, fornication, and theft that accompany huge armies (vv. 20–21).

War and its tragic consequences have been described in this first moment of the second "woe". War brings about the death of a third of humankind. But unrepentant human beings continue to inflict death, falsehood, and suffering upon one another. This is not an apocalyptic "sign" of the end of time. It is a description of the perennial evil situation of warfare among humans, from which there is no apparent escape. Only God's intervention can transform it. And God does intervene. Another mighty angel, marked by heavenly trappings, appears (10:1). He points to God's initial intervention in Israel's sacred history through the symbol of a small scroll (v. 2). The angel's great shout unleashes the seven thunders, as God has done across Israel's history (see Exod 19:19; 1 Sam 7:10; Jer 25:30; Hosea 11:10; Joel 3:16; Amos 1:2; 3:8). But what the thunders reveal is not yet to be written down (vv. 3–4). There is a sense of *waiting* in the episode.

From a position of universal authority, right hand raised to heaven, this angel utters a confession and swears an oath by the eternal God (vv. 5–6ab). The waiting is almost over (v. 6c). The promises of the prophets will be realised at the blowing of the

seventh trumpet "the mystery of God will be fulfilled" (v. 7).

The scroll indicates divine intervention, as was already the case with the scroll that only the Lamb was worthy to open (5:9–10). But this scroll is different. It is "small" and already open, a symbol of God's saving presence in Israel. Eating the scroll produces initial sweetness, but it turns bitter in the stomach. By means of these images, rewriting Ezekiel 3:1–3, John indicates the graciousness of God's presence in sacred history, yet to be fulfilled. That will take place as the seventh trumpet is blown (11:15–19). Ezekiel, who had also been given a scroll, had been instructed to "speak to the house of Israel" (Ezek 3:1). The prophecy that John will shortly utter is to be directed to all nations (Rev 10:11).

The final moment in the blowing of the sixth trumpet reveals God's presence in Israel's temple (11:1–2), and in the Law and the prophets (vv. 3–14). The measuring of the temple indicates God's love for the nation. God dwelt in the temple; the prayers of Israel's cult rose from its altar (v. 1. See also 8:3–5). But they are limited. John is not to measure the court outside the temple, "given over to the nations."

Not only was the cult in the temple exclusive, but the excluded nations regularly invaded Israel, destroyed the temple and killed the people of Jerusalem. They endure suffering for the time designated by the Prophet Daniel as a period of suffering before salvation: forty-two months, a "broken" seven years (v. 2. See Dan 7:25; 12:7). The unspoken word behind this brief presentation of the ambiguity of God's presence in the temple is that such a situation will be transcended. Two witnesses, dressed as prophets, have been part of that period of suffering. They prophesy for one thousand two hundred and sixty days (= forty-two months). They are associated with the temple cult (v. 4). Part of God's initial saving presence in Israel (v. 5), they are identified as Elijah ("no rain may fall" [1 Kgs 17:1–7]) and Moses (who turned water into blood and struck with plagues [Exod 7:14–19]) (v. 6). John's focus is upon Elijah and Moses not as personalities but as symbols of the presence of the prophets and the Law in Israel. A time comes when "they have finished their testimony" (v. 7). The beast ascends from the bottomless pit and destroys them, leaving their bodies in the streets of Jerusalem, insulted, and mocked by the nations (vv. 9–10).

Like many others from Israel's sacred history, the witnesses to the Law and the messianic promises have been destroyed. They remain slain in Jerusalem – the place where their Lord was crucified – for a time of tribulation (three and a half days: the broken seven).

Judgment necessarily follows. After the time of tribulation, the breath of the life of God enters them. They are summoned. They disappear, watched by a terrified

KEY NOTES

◆ One of the highlights of the second "woe" (sixth trumpet) is the promise of a mighty angel from heaven (10:6–7).

◆ The highlight of the third "woe" (seventh trumpet) is the realisation of that promise as the twenty-four elders from before God's throne sing (11:17).

◆ This promise is realised in the death and resurrection of Jesus; we do not have to wait for the end of all time.

crowd. This is not resurrection, but God's saving authentic witnesses from Israel's sacred history. Like all the saints of Israel, they wait for the fulfilment of the mystery of God. It is near at hand.

Some of those who rejected them (v. 12c), those who dwell in the city of Jerusalem, are destroyed. Others give glory to the God of heaven (v. 13). A glory based on fear will not last. Despite those who dwell in Jerusalem's temporary conversion to God's ways, Satan continues to wage his war through his agents, leading to Jesus' death in Jerusalem.

Below: John's revelation of the New Jerusalem.

Right: *John sees the New Jerusalem* **by Julius Schnorr von Carolsfeld**

THE BLOWING OF THE SEVENTH TRUMPET: THE THIRD "WOE" (11:15–19)

At the blowing of the seventh trumpet, "the mystery of God" announced to his prophets is fulfilled (10:7). "The kingdom of the world has become the kingdom of our Lord and Messiah" (v. 15). The Messiah belongs to "the world" and its history, not to the end of time.

The members of the heavenly court (4:1–11) again fall (Greek: *epesan*) and worship (Greek: *prosekunēsan*) God, who reigns with great power (v. 17). But the blowing of the seventh trumpet remains a woe, because the establishment of God's definitive reign in and through the presence of the Messiah brings judgment: "Your wrath has come, and the time for judging the dead". Judgment is double-edged: the saints and prophets from Israel's history, and everyone else, small or great, are rewarded. But the destroyers of the earth are destroyed (v. 18).

John has taken his audience full circle. The heavenly encounter that opened his vision of the blowing of the seven trumpets described the rising of the prayers of the saints to heaven (8:2–4). But the casting down with the censer full of fire promised an end to that situation. The signs of that end were thunder, rumblings, flashes of fire and an earthquake (v. 5).

At the blowing of the seventh trumpet, access to the earthly liturgy of the temple has come to an end. The heavenly counterpart to the earthly liturgy has been transformed by the definitive establishment of God and the Messiah (11:15, 17). God's temple is open, and the ark of the covenant can be seen (v. 19a). The phenomena that opened the heavenly encounter return. "There were peals of thunder, rumblings, flashes of lightning, and an earthquake" (8:5b;11:19b).

The satanic presence of warfare (9:13–21) has been accompanied by God's patient presence in the sacred history of Israel (11:1–14) and overcome by the death and resurrection of Jesus (11:15–19).

PREPARATION FOR THE POURING OUT OF THE SEVEN BOWLS
REVELATION 12:1–14:20

The narrative space dedicated to the description of the heavenly encounter and the pouring out of the bowls in 15:1–16:21 is brief. But it is the centrepiece of a long narrative, running from 12:1–22:5. A long preparation for the pouring out of the bowls is reported in 12:1–14:20.

THE FIRST PREPARATORY VISION (12:1–18)

There are three moments in the famous passage of 12:1–18. John sees the signs of a pregnant woman and the dragon (vv. 1–6), heavenly warfare (vv. 7–12) and a resumption of encounters between the woman, now bereft of her son, and the dragon (vv. 13–18). The meaning of the passage is hotly debated. Some Christian traditions have long identified the woman clothed with the sun in v. 1 as a symbol of the Mother of Jesus. Many accept that John is using the Greco-Roman background of the myth of Leto, impregnated by Zeus and pursued by the dragon Python. But v. 9 states that the dragon is "that ancient serpent, who is called the Devil and Satan, the deceiver of the whole world". John's inspiration comes from Genesis 2–5. It captures the fall of humankind and Satan, and the consequences of these falls.

The splendid presentation of the pregnant woman – clothed with the sun, the moon at her feet and wearing a crown of stars (v. 1) – only leads to crying out and agony (v. 2). This is hardly a portrait of the Mother of Jesus. Indeed, she loses the son, eagerly sought by the dragon (v. 3). A violent verb reports that he is snatched (Greek: *ērpasthē*) to God's throne (v. 5). John has communicated, by means of these powerful symbols, humankind's loss of the glory of its original innocence. The fallen woman flees into the wilderness (Greek: *eremos*) where she is protected and nourished. The original divine potential of humankind (v. 1. See Gen 2:4b–24) has been lost, but God has prepared a place of protection and nourishment (vv. 5–6. See Gen 3:1–24).

The great red dragon is also "in heaven", along with its own potential (vv. 3–4). But war breaks

41

out. "The devil and Satan, the deceiver of the whole world", like the woman, suffers a change of place (vv. 9, 13). He and his cohort are thrown down to earth, as "there was no longer any place for them in heaven" (v. 8). Rejoicing among the saints in heaven follows. The heavenly situation has changed with the elimination of Satan and his allies. But the situation "on earth" has now also been tragically challenged as Satan dwells there (vv. 10–12).

"On earth", the dragon and the woman are now in the same location. Satan pursues the woman as she flees into the wilderness (Greek: *eremos*) a second time (vv. 13–14). The presence of the woman in the desert after the loss of her son (v. 6) and her flight into the desert to escape Satan (v. 14) have different biblical backgrounds. The woman's initial flight (vv. 5–6) reflects humankind's loss of innocence and banishment from Eden (Gen 3:24). After the dragon's fall to earth, he pursues the woman, but she is protected by God through phenomena that recall Israel's Exodus experience: God's presence with Israel in the desert (v. 14a; see Exod 19:4; Deut 32:10–11), the gifts of the quail and the manna (v. 14b; see Exod 16:1–36), and the opening of the Red Sea (v. 15; see Exod 14:21–29).

Temptation and evil have been let loose "on earth". The woman is pursued by Satan but protected by God (vv. 13–16). Initiated by the fall of humankind and the fall of Satan as reported in the Book of Genesis, the perennial situation of the temptation of humankind is exemplified by the desert experiences of the Exodus. Frustrated by this situation, the dragon went off "to make war on the rest of her children" (v. 17). In this image, John has addressed the never-ending tension that exists between humankind and the powers of evil, the source of all temptation.

One of the keys to the interpretation of the Book of Revelation is the awareness that for John there are many saints from Israel's history. They have kept God's word, and accepted the messianic prophecies. Even though they lived and died before Christ died, they have life from the saving effects of Jesus Christ's death and resurrection that cannot be tied to any time. In this sense he was "slain before the foundation of the world" (13:8).

KEY NOTES

◆ John uses the narratives of the fall of humankind and of Satan from Genesis as background for the famous "signs in heaven" of Rev 12.

◆ The splendid presentation of the woman in Rev 12:1 cannot be an image of Mary, the Mother of Jesus.

◆ In so far as it is a portrait of the glory of humankind without sin, an *application* of the text to Mary is possible, in the light of later Catholic teaching.

◆ The use of narratives from the Book of Exodus serves John to address humankind's never-ending situation of ambiguity and temptation.

Second preparatory vision (13:1–18)

Satan takes up a position of authority between the land and the sea (12:18). From there he commissions his agents. He sees to the rising of the beast from the sea, an allusion to Daniel 7:2. The first beast represents corrupt political authority (13:1–10). A second beast is from the land. The conduct of the second beast shows that it represents corrupt religious authority (vv. 11–18). The two beasts collude so that they might corrupt "all the inhabitants of the earth" (v. 18). The beast from the earth works that all might bear the mark of the beast from the sea either on the right hand or on the forehead (vv. 16–17). It colludes with the first beast but is selfishly looking after itself (v. 12).

From the beginning of all time, Satan has pursued humankind through his agents. Some have resisted. Their names are "written in the book of life of the Lamb that was slaughtered from the foundation of the world" (v. 8). They are the saints of Israel who lived according to God's word and accepted the messianic promises of the prophets "from the foundation of the world" (see Dan 7:15–27; 9:5–6, 10). Not only have the powers of evil been rampant from all time, but the saving effects of the death and resurrection of Jesus Christ have also been present from all time. For the Christian audience of John's book, those that bear the mark of the beast are destined to never-ending and unresolvable frustration: 666 (v. 18). The collusion between corrupt political and religious authorities have always delivered the suffering, pain, and death

Far left top: *The Great Red Dragon and the Woman Clothed with the Sun (Rev. 12: 1–4)* **by William Blake**

Far left bottom: *The Fall and Expulsion from Garden of Eden* **by Michelangelo**

Above: Lamb of God (Agnus Dei) mosaic in the Martini church in Braunschweig, Niedersachsen, Germany

KEY NOTES

◆ John uses the two beasts to point to the perennial sources of evil in the world.

◆ The beast from the sea refers to corrupt political authority that has been present throughout human history.

◆ The beast from the land refers to religious authorities who can do wonderful signs, and raise up statues, in collaboration with corrupt political authority.

◆ Equally present to the whole of human history are the saving effects of the death and resurrection of Jesus, slain "from the foundation of the world" (13:8).

that results from the lordship of evil. For the early Christians, the collusion between Roman authorities (political) and Jewish leadership (religious) resulted in the death of Jesus. But the effects of the death and resurrection of Jesus Christ have set up an alternative lordship for those who do not bear the mark of the beast.

Third preparatory vision (14:1–20)

Two major moments are narrated in the visions of 14:1–20. In 14:1–5, the Lamb is surrounded by the first fruits of his being slain yet standing, his death and resurrection: 144,000 from Israel who have been faithful to the Law and the Prophets. They are "the first fruits of the Lamb" (v. 4). The theme of this final preparatory vision is stated: God has made salvation possible from all times because of the death and resurrection of the Lamb (13:8).

A longer section is dedicated to a description of the final victory of the one like the Son of Man, and the judgment that comes with that victory (vv. 6–20). The figure of the Son of Man, with a golden crown on his head and a sharp sickle in his hand, is located at the centre of the passage (v. 14). He dominates the two sets of three angels that surround him in vv. 6–13 and vv. 15–20.

From vv. 6–13, three angels introduce him, announcing that the hour for his victory has come (first angel: vv. 6–7), the fall of Babylon (second angel: v. 8), and the torment of those who have worshiped the beast, matched by the blessedness of those already

saved in the time of Israel (third angel: vv. 9–13).

After the dominant appearance of the one like the Son of Man among his angels (v. 14), three further angels enter the vision in vv. 15–20. These angels announce even more precisely, the nature of the victory of the one like the Son of Man and its consequences. Isaiah 63:6–7 used a vision of a winepress as a symbol of condemnation. Divine punishment crushes and destroys the unfaithful.

The theme of judgment remains in Revelation 14:15–20, but John imaginatively reinterprets the winepress to also describe the saving effects of the blood of Jesus. The hour for the victory of the one like the Son of Man has come (first angel: vv. 15–16), another angel joins the harvesting, sickle in hand (second angel: v. 17), and the vintage is gathered "outside the city", recalling the location of Jesus' death. The vintage produces a life-giving blood that covers the earth (third angel: vv. 18–20).

The saving effects of Jesus' death and resurrection have been perennially available (vv. 1–5; see 13:8). The historical event of Jesus' execution "outside the city" generated a universal saving flow of blood (vv. 6–20). The death of Christ appears as the judgment of God in its dual aspect: the gathering of the elect (reaping) and the condemnation and destruction of the evil forces (the vintage and the pressing of the grapes).

The scene has been set for the final encounter between God, creator and saviour, and the powers of evil at Harmagedon (15:1–16:21).

KEY NOTES

- John insists that the saints of Israel have been saved by the effects of Jesus' death and resurrection.

- Jesus, the one like the Son of Man, dominates and judges all history.

- The three angels who introduce the one like the Son of Man, and the further three angels that follow his presentation, judge the good and the wicked.

- The judgment executed by the one like the Son of Man brings destruction for the wicked and salvation for those who are touched by the saving effects of his blood.

THE POURING OUT OF THE SEVEN BOWLS
REVELATION 15:1–16:21

THE HEAVENLY ENCOUNTER: 15:1–8

John sees a final "sign in heaven" announcing that events are coming to an end. He sees seven angels with seven plagues. They are "the last" (Greek: *tas eschatas*). When the plagues are poured out, "the wrath of God is ended" (v. 1. Greek: *etelesthē*). This passage will close pointing to a time when "the seven plagues of the seven angels were ended" (v. 8. Greek: *telesthōsin*).

John sees "those who had conquered the beast and its image and the number of its name" (v. 2). They are the saints of Israel, the 144,000 from the tribes of Israel in the sixth seal (7:1–8), and the 144,000 who stand on Mount Zion with the Lamb (14:1–5). Like the Lamb (5:6; 14:1), and the two witnesses (11:11), they have returned to life despite violent execution. The sea of glass, described during the heavenly liturgy of 4:6, is now "mixed with fire", the result of the fallen angels of the fourth trumpet casting fire upon the sea and the land (8:7–12). The saints have endured the ambiguity of Israel's history, a blend of God-given human potential and the presence of the Satanic.

Harps of God in their hands, the saints sing the song of Moses, the prophet who gave Israel the Law, and of the Lamb who brought that era to closure (v. 3). Representatives of both eras praise God as King of the nations, the one who will see to the fulfilment of the messianic promises. God's justice and judgment will be exercised (v. 4).

The rest of the heavenly vision describes the commissioning of the seven angels who exit from the open temple (v. 5). The bright linen robes and the gold sashes highlight their heavenly origins (v. 6). One of the four living creatures from before the throne of God (4:6) gives them the bowls from which the plagues will be poured. The glory of God fills the empty temple. The consecration of the temples of Moses and Solomon was marked by the presence of God's glory (see Exod 40:32–38; 1 Kings 8:10–11; 1 Chr 5:13–14; 7:1–3).

But they marked the beginnings of God's presence in the Jerusalem temple. For John, until the pouring out of the seven plagues is finished, the presence of the glory of God in the heavenly temple prevents anyone from entering the temple (v. 8). The heavenly counterpart of the Jerusalem temple has been emptied. No further mention is made of the temple until John's description of the New Jerusalem (21:3–4, 22). One era in God's dealings with humankind is coming to an end as Jerusalem's temple comes to an end. "No one could enter" the heavenly temple because the usefulness of the Jerusalem temple as access to God *is coming to an end*. A new era begins; the temple "is the Lord God almighty and the Lamb" (21:22).

KEY NOTES

◆ The theme of "the end" is stated three times in the heavenly encounter of Rev 15:1–8.

◆ This theme does not mean the end of the world or the end of the history, but the end of the traditional way to God, so dear to the saints of Israel: the temple.

◆ Revelation and the Gospels interpret the death and resurrection of Jesus as the end of the era of access to God through the temple.

THE POURING OUT OF THE SEVEN BOWLS: 16:1–21

The bowls, like the other "sevens", are poured out in a pattern of 4 + 3.

THE POURING OUT OF THE FIRST FOUR BOWLS (16:1–9)

A loud voice from the empty temple commands the angels to pour out the seven bowls of the wrath of God (16:1). The pouring out of the first four bowls recalls the plagues of Egypt, destructive events that led to freedom. They punish the unrepentant worshippers of the beast from the sea.

The pouring out of the first bowl produces "a foul and painful sore" (Exod 9:8–12 [the sixth plague in Egypt]) on those who had the mark of the beast and worshipped his image (Rev 13:16; 14:9) They have given themselves over to evil and sinfulness, the fruit of corrupt political and religious authority. They are condemned to failure in the eyes of God.

The pouring out of the second bowl transforms the sea into something like the "blood of a corpse" (see Exod 7:17–24 [the fourth plague in Egypt]). "Every living thing in the sea died" (Rev 16:3).

Far left: *The Forerunners of Christ with Saints and Martyrs* **by Fra Angelico**

Below: Model of the City of David, Jerusalem in the late Second Temple period; located in Israel Museum, Jerusalem

The pouring out of the third bowl continues the administration of the poisoning of the waters as they are turned into blood. The satanic powers cast down into the abyss (9:1–2) and the beast that rose out of the sea (13:1) are destroyed. They were responsible for the shedding of "the blood of the saints and the prophets". The angel of the waters, supported by the altar of the temple, insists that God's justice is righteously exercised in their destruction by blood (vv. 5–6).

The pouring out of the fourth bowl results in a scorching heat from the sun (see Exod 9:22–26 [the eighth plague in Egypt]). The sinfulness, destruction, and ambiguity of the human situation are judged by God. Ambiguity is uncovered (Rev 16:8–9a). But, like the Pharaohs in Egypt, they do not repent. On the contrary, they continue to "curse the name of God" (v. 9b).

John selects from the plagues of Egypt to describe God's

Above: Crucifixion from the East Window in St Chad's, Dunholme, 1901

judgment upon the origins of sin and evil in the world. This judgment takes place in the death and resurrection of Jesus, soon to be symbolically reported in vv. 10–21. But, as is evident throughout history, sin, destruction and the ambiguity of the human situation continue to exist. Believers who live in the period after God's saving and judging action in the death and resurrection of Jesus Christ must recognise that many, in different ways, continue to curse the name of God. The Book of Revelation was written to dissuade Christians from joining them!

The pouring out of the final three bowls brings judgment and destruction upon the kingdom of the beast.

The pouring out of the fifth bowl (16:10–11)

The fifth plague is poured out upon the throne of the beast (v. 10). The symbol of its authority is destroyed. Those in its kingdom, in complete darkness, gnaw their tongues in agony, producing pains and sores (v. 11). The authority of Satan is being steadily overcome as God's wrath is poured out. But there is no conversion. They do not repent (v. 11).

Tel Megiddo National Park, Israel

The pouring out of the sixth bowl (16:12–16)

As with the seals and the trumpets, the pouring out of the sixth bowl leads toward the climax of the series. Recalling the release of the four powers at the Euphrates at the blowing of the sixth trumpet (9:14), the river is dried up to enhance the gathering of a huge force. It is made up of the powers of evil: three foul spirits like frogs, agents of the dragon, the beast from the sea, and the beast from the land (16:13). These demonic spirits, performing signs, gather a huge army from the kings of the earth to do battle "on the great day of the Lord" (v. 14). Battle lines are drawn.

Without introduction, a voice recalling words of Jesus and earlier promises intervenes. He is coming suddenly, like a thief (see Matt 24:43; Luke 12:39). The battle of the Harmagadon is not about the end of all time. It will be a definitive and final encounter between the forces of evil (vv. 13–14) and the authority of God (vv. 17–21). Those who have resisted evil, remained clothed and walked worthily with Jesus Christ are blessed (v. 15. See 3:4: "a few persons in Sardis who have not soiled their clothes; they will walk with me, dressed in white, for they are worthy"). They have no cause to fear the outcome of the great battle.

The Hebrew name for the battlefield is Harmagadon (v. 16). It is best translated as "the mountain of Megiddo". Although not a mountain, the city of Megiddo was the site of several famous battles (see Judg 5:19; 2 Chron 35:22). The most just and God-fearing king of Judah, Josiah, was slain there by the Egyptian Necho II in 609 BCE. As with the loss of Israel's holiest king at Megiddo, the death of Jesus appeared to be a victory for the corrupt authorities assembled by the agents of Satan (vv. 13–14). As the audience will learn in vv. 17–21, such was not the case.

Associating himself with the Christian tradition that Jesus was executed on a mountain outside the city of Jerusalem (see John 19:20; Heb 13:12), John turns the city of Megiddo into "Mount Megiddo", Harmagedon in Hebrew. The death of Jesus took place on the mountain of Calvary. It was the fruit of a "great battle on the day of the Lord" (v. 14). It brings judgment between good and evil (v. 15).

The pouring out of the seventh bowl (16:17–21)

The pouring out of the seventh bowl reports the result of the great battle at Harmagedon. The bowl is poured "into the air", indicating the universal significance of what has taken place. The voice of God from the throne and the temple announces: "It is done!" (v. 17. Greek: *gegonen*). In the heavenly encounter that introduced the pouring out of the seven bowls, John heard that the end was at hand (15:1 [twice], 8). The voice of God now announces that it has happened. Although from different authors, directed to different audiences, there is a parallel with Jesus' final word on the cross in the Gospel of John: "It is finished" (John 19:30: Greek: *tetelestai*). Jesus Christ's response to God has been completed, and all evil has been overcome. End-time language

The combination of allusions to the Book of Exodus and the destruction of evil indicates that good will emerge from destruction.

KEY NOTES

- The punishment that flows from God's just judgment does not produce repentance.

- The forces of evil gather for a final battle at Harmagedon.

- The name Harmagedon alludes to the execution of Jesus "outside the city" in Jerusalem.

- The single Greek word for "it is finished" (*gegonen*) uttered by the loud voice from heaven spells out the victory of God in and through the death and resurrection of Jesus.

- All evil, including Jerusalem/Babylon, is destroyed, but they only curse God.

- This message still retains its relevance in an entirely self-sufficient world, where no spirituality exists.

of lightning, rumblings, peals of thunder and an earthquake is used to describe the effects of this victory. But they do not point to an end time. This language recaptures the results of the revelation of the mystery of God at the blowing of the seventh seal (v. 18. See 11:19). The Synoptic Gospels, and especially the Gospel of Matthew, use end-time language to indicate that the death of Jesus marks the turning point of the ages (see Matt 27:43–54. See also Mark 15:33–39; Luke 23:44–47). John repeats that tradition.

Babylon is split into three parts. The prophet Ezekiel 5:1–4 provided John with a sign to tell of the destruction of Jerusalem. He was instructed to shave his head and beard, and to weigh the hair (v. 1). The hair was to be made into three bundles: "One third of the hair you shall burn … one third you shall take and strike with the sword … one third you will scatter to the wind" (vv. 2–3).

Ezekiel's comment on the destruction of Jerusalem is now applied to Babylon/Jerusalem: "This is Jerusalem; I have set her in the centre of the nations, with countries all around her. But she has rebelled against my ordinances and my statutes… Thus says the Lord God: I, I myself am coming against you; I will execute judgments among you in the sight of the nations" (vv. 5–6, 8).

The earthquake described in Rev 16:17–21, however, is more destructive than all other earthquakes. Such an occurrence had never been seen before (v. 18). As well as dividing Jerusalem into three, it destroys all the cities of the nations, the islands and the mountains. Jesus' death and resurrection brings universal judgment (vv. 19–20).

Those upon whom the huge hailstones fell, however, "cursed God for the plague of the hail, so fearful was that plague" (v. 21). The judgment upon evil enacted at the crucifixion does not lead to conversion. John asks Christian audiences of all ages and situations to be aware that they live in a world where sinfulness continues to threaten.

Each of the "sevens" has described "the mystery of God" (10:7). The announcement of the definitive completion of God's design, and the judgment that flows from it, climaxes in the pouring out of the seventh bowl (16:17–21).

Left: *Angel with Seven Jars containing the Wrath of God*, fresco in Padua baptistery by Menabuoi

Far right: *Christ on a White Horse* by Gebhard Fugel (1863–1939)

CONSEQUENCES OF THE POURING OUT OF THE SEVEN BOWLS
REVELATION 17:1–22:5

A "bird's-eye view" of 17:1–22:5 shows that narrative follows the same pattern as 14:6–20. There one like the Son of Man was at the centre of the passage (14:14), accompanied by three angels before (vv. 6, 8, 9) and three angels after (vv. 15, 17, 18) his majestic presence is recorded (v. 14). Revelation 17:1–22:5 is identical, even though the narrative is told at a greater length. The Word of God is at the centre of two sets of three angels, as shown in the table below.

Angels who had one of the seven bowls (15:1, 7) appear as the first (17:1) and the last (21:9) of the six angels. Within that narrative, John unfolds the three consequences of the victory of Harmagedon: Babylon, the locus of all evil, is destroyed (17:1–19:10), all evil powers are destroyed or rendered powerless (19:11–21:8), and the chosen are gathered (21:9–22:5).

17:1–18: An angel who had one of the seven bowls shows John the judgment on the "great whore"

    18:1–20: An angel announces the fall of Babylon

        18:21–19:10: An angel announces the humiliation of Babylon

            19:11–16: The Word on a white horse is victorious over the nations

        19:17–21: An angel announces the destruction of all wicked powers

    20:1–21:8: An angel binds Satan for a thousand years

21:9–22:5: An angel who had one of the seven bowls invites John to witness the "bride of the Lamb" and the river of life.

REVELATION 17:7–14

Interpreters puzzle over the exact identity of elements in 17:7–14: the seven mountains on which the woman is seated, the seven kings and their history, the ten further kings who receive their authority from the first seven kings. They cannot be identified with certainty. The use of the numbers "seven" and "ten" points to their symbolic meaning. Those gathered in vv. 7–14 are the forces of evil, assembling to make war on the Lamb.

THE SEVEN MOUNTAINS

Many interpret the image of the woman as seated on seven mountains in 17:9 as Rome. This leads to the improbable destruction of Rome by Rome, as the beast of vv. 15–18 is also identified with Rome. But Rome was never described as located on "seven mountains". On the other hand, in Jewish apocalyptic writings (1 Enoch 24:3–4), Jerusalem is described as "seven mountains." Thus, vv. 15–18 records the corrupt political authority of Rome destroying the city of Jerusalem in 70 CE.

Right: Gaius Iulius Caesar in Rome, Italy

Vision of the first consequence: 17:1–19:10

Not without its obscurities, 17:1–19:10 describes the destruction of Babylon/Jerusalem (17:1–18), the lament over its destruction (18:1–20), the rejoicing of heaven, and the marriage of the Lamb (19:1–10). Despite long-held conviction that the beast with whom the woman shares abominable intimacy is Rome (17:7–14), the message is more universal. The woman is a symbol of Jerusalem, "the great city" (v. 18) whose long collusion with evil political and religious authorities led to the execution of Jesus. She is now destroyed, and the "words of God" are fulfilled (vv. 15–18). All who have profited from the prostitution of the woman lament (18:1–24), while "the prophets and saints" of Israel whose blood has been shed in Jerusalem (v. 24) can rejoice as God has given judgment for them against that city (v. 20). Heaven rejoices, the marriage of the Lamb has come, and the bride of the Lamb makes herself ready (19:7).

As this passage opened, the ambiguity of "the woman" we first met in 12:1–18 (Greek: *hē gynē*) was negatively resolved in 17:1–6. There she was mounted on the beast (Greek: *hē gynē*). It will be positively resolved in the marriage of the Lamb, announced (but not enacted) as the passage closes in 19:6–9 (Greek: *hē gynē*). It will be enacted in the first words of the final consequence (21:9–10).

Vision of the second consequence: 19:11–21:8

The second consequence of Harmagedon is the destruction of all wicked powers (19:11–21:8). It opens with a description of the fierce rider on the white horse whose name is not known (19:11–12), but whose function is clear. He brings integrity (v. 11), makes God known (v. 13) and executes judgment (v. 15). Accompanied by a heavenly army, he exercises his messianic authority through the shedding of his blood (v. 13a, v. 15). Through the cross he is established as King of kings and Lord of lords (v. 16). John describes, separately, two aspects of the righteous war against all evil (19:17–21 and 20:7–10). Each aspect of the battle is followed by judgment (20:1–6 and 20:11–21:8).

In the first aspect of the battle, the destruction of the forces of evil begins (19:17–21). The beast from the sea and his false prophet (the beast from the land of 13:11–18) are "thrown down alive [Greek: *zōntes*: "living"] into the lake of fire that burns with sulphur" (19:20). All the rest (vv. 17b–19) are destroyed by the rider on the horse (v. 21).

Judgment follows. Satan has fallen (9:1–12; 12:7–12). He must exercise his corrupting power through his agents (see 12:13–13:18). "That ancient serpent, who is the devil and Satan" (20:2; see 12:9) has

KEY NOTES

◆ The theme of "the woman" is strongly present across the second half of the Book of Revelation.

◆ If the woman mounted on the beast and finally destroyed is Rome, then Rome is destroying Rome.

◆ Jerusalem is described in Jewish literature as seated on seven mountains.

◆ The number "seven" associated with the kings in Rev 17 means the totality of corrupt political authorities.

◆ This universal (i.e., not just Rome) interpretation of Rev 17 makes sense of the universal lamentations of Rev 18.

KEY NOTES

- God's victory at Harmagedon (16:17–21) is described in detail: the victorious Word of God (19:11–16), and two aspects of the same battle (19:17–21 and 20:7–10).

- The two aspects of the battle focus upon the victory of the saints from Israel's history (19:17–21) and the victory of all the nations (20:7–10).

- The interpretation of "the thousand-year reign" of 20:1–6 determines the life and faith of many Christian communities who read Revelation as a Word of God describing exactly how things will be.

- Those who reign for a thousand years (a long period of time) are the saints from Israel's history.

long been rendered powerless, locked and sealed in the pit. The "thousand years" is the age that lasts from Satan's original fall until he is released (vv. 1–2). "After that he must be let out for a while" (v. 3).

The thousand years mark the period of Israel, during which Satan's agents have spread pain, warfare, death and wickedness. Those in Israel who have been slain because of their observance of the Law and the acceptance of the promises of the prophets will "reign with Christ" (vv. 4–5). They belong to "the first resurrection" and will not face "the second death" (v. 6). All others who die must wait for Christ's victory to come to life (v. 5). The second aspect of the battle is reported in 20:7–10. The Christian era, continuing God's sacred history, begins with the release of Satan (v. 7) for the definitive battle at the end of the thousand years. Recalling the description of Harmagedon (16:12–21), the battle is universal. The nations, Gog and Magog (see Ezek 38), and innumerable forces gather for the kill, but they are destroyed by fire (vv. 8–9). Thrown down, Satan joins the beast and the false prophet in the lake of fire and sulphur. They are not destroyed, but tormented day and night "forever and ever" (v. 10).

Judgment, resulting in both destruction and blessing, follows (21:11–21:8). Everyone is summoned before the one seated on the great white throne (vv. 11–14; see Dan 7:9–10). At the "second death" those whose names are not written in the book of life are cast into the lake of fire (v. 15). Those who conquer sin and evil will dwell in the New Jerusalem, a heavenly holy city like a bride adorned for her husband. God will dwell with mortals; death and suffering will be no more (21:3–4). But the place of the wicked will be in the burning lake (v. 8).

Vision of the third consequence (21:9–22:5)

The vision of the final consequence of the victory at Harmagedon (21:9) recalls the vision of the first consequence (17:1):

Then one of the seven angels who had the seven bowls came and said to me, "Come, I will show you the judgment of the great whore who is seated on many waters" (17:1).

Then one of the seven angels who had the seven bowls full of the seven last plagues came and said to me, "Come, I will show you the bride, the wife of the Lamb" (21:9).

Simple yet subtle literary techniques indicate the end of the cycle of three consequences. Recalling the seven angels who had the bowls of the seven last plagues, John links these three consequences with Harmagedon. They are the result of the angelic pouring out of the seven bowls (15:1–16:21). After the violent judgment that dominated the first two consequences, the third reports the gift of the New Jerusalem (21:9–22:5).

THE LETTERS AND THE NEW JERUSALEM

The promises to the victors in the Letters are fulfilled in the New Jerusalem.
For example, the believers at Ephesus were promised access to the tree of life (2:7).
The tree of life is found in the New Jerusalem (22:2).
The believers at Pergamum were promised a white stone (2:17),
fulfilled in the brilliant stones of the New Jerusalem.
The promise to the faithful in Laodicea that they would
sit down on Christ's throne (3:21) is fulfilled in 22:1–2.
The potential of the local churches is realised in the New Jerusalem,
the Church as it should be.

THE THOUSAND-YEAR REIGN

Rev 20:1–6 has puzzled interpreters from earliest times. Some contemporary communities read the biblical text as an exact indication of what will happen to Christians. Most claim that the thousand years is the time from Jesus Christ's historical presence until the final judgment. Others claim that there will be a golden age of faith on earth before the final judgment (*Postmillennialism*). For some, the period belongs to those in the Church and in heaven before the general resurrection, after which they will enjoy final bliss (*Amillennialism*). A further suggestion is that Jesus Christ will return prior to the final inauguration of a thousand years of peace *(Premillennialism)*. An extreme interpretation claims at an unknown time there will be a "rapture". Christian believers who are alive will be gathered with all risen believers and they will meet the Lord in the air. All others will be "left behind". This *Friendly Guide* claims that the thousand years is a round number for the period of Israel's history when the saints of Israel are already saved. They will face no judgment. At the end of that period, Satan is let loose to engage in a final conflict with Jesus Christ. It took place in Jesus' death and resurrection. Satan was defeated (19:17–21; 20:7–10).

KEY NOTES

◆ The repetition of the number "twelve," closing with the names of the twelve apostles of the Lamb in the description of the "holy city of Jerusalem", links the New Jerusalem with the Christian Church.

◆ The promises to the seven imperfect churches in the letters of 2:1–3:22 are fulfilled in the descriptions of the New Jerusalem of 21:9–22:5.

◆ The New Jerusalem has no further need for a temple.

◆ God and the Lamb are present in the New Jerusalem.

Below: *Woman Clothed with the Sun* **from Bodleian Ms 150**

Right: *Scene from the Apocalypse* **by Francis Danby**

The angel shows John the bride of the Lamb, his wife (21:9: the wife and the bride [*hē gynē*] of the Lamb). The bride is the heavenly Jerusalem, coming down from heaven (v. 10). Her description is highlighted by a structure based upon the number twelve and light-filled embellishment (vv. 11–21). The spectacular (and impossible) description of the structure of the New Jerusalem points to the spiritual reality of the Christian Church, built upon the story of Israel with the foundation of the 12 apostles. At the beginning of his book, John wrote letters to seven fragile churches in Asia, exhorting them to overcome their temptations to consort with the social and religious practices of the Greco-Roman world (2:1–3:22). He closes his book by symbolically describing the ideal and spiritual reality of the Christian Church – as it should be (21:9–22:5).

The ambiguous situation of the woman in 12:13–18 was resolved by the whore mounted on and destroyed by the beast (17:1–6, 15–18). But a third possibility now emerges: the woman (*hē gynē*) united in marriage as the bride of the Lamb. The ambiguity (12:1–18) and the sinfulness (17:1–18) of the human condition has been overcome by the death and resurrection of Jesus. Rejecting the attractions of the powers of evil still rampant in society, humankind enjoys life and light in the New Jerusalem (22:1–5).

All whose names are written in the Lamb's book of life will dwell in the city where its temple is the Lord God and the Lamb. There "the glory of God is its light, and its lamp is the Lamb" (vv. 22–23). There is no longer need for the physical temple in Jerusalem. It has been replaced and transcended in the new era that had its beginnings in the death and resurrection of Jesus (see Mark 11:20–25; 15:38–39; Matt 25:51–54; Luke 23:45).

All nations will stream to it, but those who practice abomination or falsehood are excluded (vv. 24–27). John tells of the life-giving water and tree of life (22:1–5). The nations will be healed, the servants of the Lamb, marked by his sign, will worship. There will be no more night. "The Lord God will be their light, and they will reign forever and ever" (v. 5).

THE EPILOGUE
REVELATION 22:6–21

John closes his book with two literary chiasms (vv. 6–9 and vv. 10–17), a final warning and a promise from Jesus Christ (vv. 18–20a) and the author's response (vv. 20b–21). John recalls the prologue as he opens his first chiasm insisting, "These words are trustworthy and true, for the Lord, the God of the spirits of the prophets has sent his angel to show his servants what must take place quickly" (22:6. See 1:1).

At the centre of the chiasm, Jesus speaks, guaranteeing his coming and blessing those who keep the words that they have just encountered, interpreting "this book" (22:7).

The chiasm closes with a final interaction between John and the angel who has shown John "these things". The era of the angel's ministry to John, and John's submission to the angel are over. They are equals. Only one thing matters: God must be worshipped (vv. 8–9).

Dialogue between the angels and John continues as the second chiasm opens. The former insists that the latter not seal up the message contained in "this book" as Jesus comes quickly. Nevertheless, a world marked by sin and goodness endures: "Let the evildoer still do evil, and the filthy still be filthy, and the righteous still do right, and the holy still be holy" (vv. 10–11).

Repeating the centre of the first chiasm, Jesus again speaks. He guarantees his coming and his judgment (v. 12). He is the Lord of all history (v. 13). He proclaims that those who have washed their robes and thus enter the New Jerusalem are blessed (v. 14).

CHIASM
The word "chiasm" is used to describe a widespread literary practice, even in contemporary writing. It is also called "a sandwich construction". A passage is made up of three parts. The first part matches the third, and a substantial contribution to the overall argument of the passage is found in the centre of the "chiasm". Rev. 22:6–9 and 10–17 are good examples of this practice. The two slices of bread are on the outside, and the heart of the message is between them.

Jesus continues to speak as the second chiasm closes. He repeats the warning about the ambiguity of the world into which "this book" is sent. "Outside are the dogs and sorcerers and fornicators and murderers and idolaters, and everyone who loves and practices falsehood" (v. 15).

The insistence upon the ongoing sinfulness that surrounds the audience of "this book" in vv. 10–11 and v. 15 is a powerful indication that the Book of Revelation is not about the end of the world. It is addressed to Christians living in an ambiguous world, where the believers must cope with the attractive but destructive practices of a world foreign to the way of Jesus, the root and descendent of David (v. 16). Angelic mediation has ceased, as the Spirit and the bride summon the audience: "Come." They must pass it on, repeating the command, "Come" (v. 17). The gift of the water of life can be theirs.

The first chiasm closed with the command: "Worship God" (v. 10). The second chiasm closes with the invitation: "Come" (v. 17).

One of the strangest warnings in the Bible appears in vv. 18–19. John warns that the authoritative words of prophecy found in "this book" must never be altered. Anyone who does so will be punished by the plagues described in the book, and the loss of a share in the tree of life and the holy city. Never has a biblical author claimed such authority for his own writing. Neither does John!

The continual use of "this book" throughout 22:6–19 (seven times) looks beyond John's own book to the Sacred Scriptures of Israel that John has used throughout to instruct struggling Christians in Asia Minor. No doubt he regarded his own writing as important. But it was not *his book* that could bear no alteration. That dignity, because it articulated God's design from all time and until the end of all time (God and Jesus are the Alpha and the Omega), belongs only to the Sacred Scriptures of Israel, the Word of God.

"For John the Christ-event is the key to understanding the [Old Testament], and yet reflection on the OT context leads the way to further comprehension of this event…"⁵

The Book of Revelation can now close with the promise of Jesus: "Surely I am coming quickly" (v. 20a). Making use of an acclamation that was apparently widespread in the early Church (see 1 Cor 16:22), John replies: "So be it! Come Lord Jesus" (v. 20b). The Book of Revelation may be dominated by a belief that the death and resurrection has already freed believers from sin and death. But John accepts and continues the tradition that there will be a final coming of Jesus. His book may not be a description of that moment, as many believe, but he remains firmly within that Christian view of history.

A long journey through history may lie ahead. Thus, he adopts a formula widely used in New Testament letters to pray for that journey (see Col 4:18; Heb 13:25; 1 Tim 6:21; 2 Tim 4:22; Titus 3:15). He asks that the grace of the Lord Jesus may accompany his audience of all ages along their journey into the future. Challenges lie ahead, but John asks that his audience be comforted by the fact that they dwell in the New Jerusalem, made possible by the death and resurrection of Jesus (v. 21).

Far left: *Christ with Seven Candlesticks,* **from the Goslar Cemetery for the Fallen in Hildersheim**

KEY NOTES

- The epilogue (Rev 22:6–21) recaptures much of what was said in the prologue (1:1–8).

- The closing page of the Book of Revelation makes it clear that the world is not ending. It must face a future where sin and goodness exist side by side.

- "This book" is not the Book of Revelation, but Israel's Sacred Scriptures.

- John continues to insist upon the traditional Christian view of Jesus' coming at the end of time.

- His book, however, was written to guide believers through a long journey that may lie ahead, before the final appearance of the Alpha and Omega of history.

A FINAL WORD

The worldwide pandemic of COVID-19 has led many to have recourse to the Book of Revelation for imagery, and even a theology, that explains what God might be doing in our third Christian millennium. As you are aware, now that we have come to the end of our *Friendly Guide*, this is an abuse of John's book. What we have shared across these pages is part of a movement among New Testament interpreters called a "new look" in Revelation studies. It challenges the interpretation of Revelation as a series of symbolic representations of the end of all time, almost unquestionably accepted since the time of St Augustine's *City of God* in 426 CE.

Patmos was not a penal settlement. Domitian did not systematically persecute Christians in Asia at the end of the first Christian century. Nor were Christians being forced to participate in the Roman Emperor cults. Babylon is a symbol of unfaithful Jerusalem, not the city of Rome. More positively, Revelation was written to Christians who are "a kingdom, priests serving his [Christ's] God and Father" (Rev 1:6. See 5:10). The victory of the death and resurrection of Jesus over the perennial presence of evil is proclaimed throughout the document (5:6, 9–14; 7:12–8:1; 11:15–19; 16:17–21; 18:20–24; 19:1–8, 17–21; 21:11–15; 21:1–22:5). Rampant evil is powerfully and frighteningly described with biblical and apocalyptic language. But the same language is used to claim that evil has been definitively overcome in and through the death and resurrection of Jesus.

"The saints" are all those in Israel, described in Daniel 7:23–27 (and elsewhere), who have lived by the Word of God and accepted the messianic promises of the prophets (8:3–4; 11:18; 13:7, 10; 14:12; 16:6; 17:6; 18:20). They already have life, fruit of the saving effects of the death and resurrection of Jesus "from the foundation of the world" (13:8). John presents the model of those saints from Israel's history to guide Asian Christians, tempted by the allure of the Greco-Roman world and its pagan way of life. He invites them away from their mediocrity (2:1–3:22) into the life and light of the New Jerusalem, the Christian Church (22:1–5).

Times and literary practices have changed since the 90s of the first Christian century. But the conflict between ambiguous and destructive evil and the light of God's saving presence among us is alive and well. We are experiencing it in our own challenging times. John tells us where we should place our trust.

GLOSSARY

A thousand years: Rev 20:1–3 tells of the binding of Satan in a bottomless pit for a thousand years, at the end of which Satan will be let out "for a little while". Interpretation of the thousand years has led to many understandings of a Satan-free thousand years, the main ones being Amillennialism, Postmillennialism and Premillennialism (see elsewhere in the Glossary).

Amillennialism: The belief that Rev 20:1–3 refers to a symbolic long period that matches the period of the Church on earth and the saints in heaven. This indefinite period will lead to the final bliss of all the righteous after the general resurrection.

Angels: As agents that communicate between God and humankind, angels play important roles in apocalyptic literature. Very often an angel is needed to explain the strange narratives and symbols. This figure is called "the interpreting angel". In John's Revelation, the angels are often used to represent God's initial revelation through Israel's Sacred Scriptures.

Apocalypse: A Greek word (*apokalypsis*) used to describe a literature that had its beginnings in Israel's Sacred Scriptures and gathered strength among both Jewish and Christian authors in the early Christian era. The word means "revelation" or "unveiling", and the literature grew in minority groups in times of unwinnable conflict. Religious apocalypses (Jewish or Christian) teach that God will bring history to an end, destroying the wicked and blessing the holy.

Apocalyptic: An adjective used for the characteristic literary features of an *apocalypse*. As God is the active character, overcoming evil and blessing holiness, symbols and strange non-earthly narratives describe that conflict. God's action cannot be described with normal stories. The word is regularly associated with "eschatology" (i.e., apocalyptic eschatology) to refer to a particular way of interpreting the end-time events (see "eschatology").

Above: Angels from Banska Stiavnica

Colours: John regularly uses colours to communicate meanings. Most importantly, gold and white point to the divine sphere. Warfare, violence, and death are communicated through the colours red, black, and pale green.

Cult: A technical word that refers to the ritual actions, usually administered by a priestly caste, that take place in a sacred space to honour and praise God. For Jews, the central location for cultic activities was the temple in Jerusalem. John transcends earthly cult with the presence of God and the Lamb in the New Jerusalem (Rev 21:22).

Epilogue: A passage that ends a long narrative, drama or other form of communication. It is normally used to look back across the communication, often summarising in a way that recalls the prologue. Authors often use an epilogue to salute their audience.

Eschatology: An all-encompassing expression associated with events that come at the end of time, from the plural Greek word *ta eschata*, meaning the "last things" or the "last times". Its adjective is "eschatological".

Exodus experience: According to the Book of Exodus, many spectacular events accompanied the liberation of Israel from Egypt, and the journey of the people through the desert to the Promised Land: the ten plagues, the crossing of the Red Sea, the manna from heaven, the quail in the desert, the column of light that led the people during the night, etc. John uses some of these experiences to tell of God's victory over evil, especially imagery that comes from the ten plagues of Exodus 4–12.

Fornication: The first level of meaning of this word is illicit sexual relations. Some interpreters accept that John exhorts his audience to sexual purity. In fact, following the example of Israel's prophets (esp. Isaiah, Jeremiah, and Ezekiel), he uses it to condemn his audience's temptation to compromise themselves with the false Gods of the Greco-Roman world, including Emperor worship.

Gog and Magog: These names come to John from Ezekiel 38:1–6, but they do not indicate geographical locations. In Rev 20:7–10, John describes the final stage of the battle between God and evil. Gog and Magog are "the nations of the four corners of the earth" that have succumbed to the deception of Satan (20:8). They are defeated by God's intervention in Jesus' death and resurrection.

Greco-Roman: The Greek language, culture, customs, religions and practices dominated the Mediterranean world for many centuries before the rise of the Roman empire. Most literate people in the region spoke Greek rather than Latin. The Romans adopted, and adapted, Greek ways. They added some of their own customs and practices. This mixed culture of Greek and Roman ways is referred to as "Greco-Roman".

Hades: The Greek God of the underworld gave his name to the location of the dead, already widely referred to as "Hades" in Greek literature well before Christian times. It is parallel to the Hebrew "Sheol". It was a place of darkness and shadow, where Hades ruled, from which there was no exit (with a few exceptions in Greek mythology).

Harmagedon: This strange word appears in Rev 16:16. It has been formed by joining the Hebrew word for "mountain" (*har*) to the name of a famous battle site in northern Israel, Megiddo (see "Megiddo"). In contemporary culture it has become the widely-used "Armageddon" of films and literature.

Marah: A Hebrew word meaning "bitter". On their journey out of Egypt, the Israelites reach the well of bitter water (Exod 15:23–24). Suffering from

Above: A modern "golden age"

lack of water and lack of food, the Israelites complain against Moses. He resolves the situation by rendering the water sweet by throwing a piece of wood into the well, promising better times to those who obey the commandments. He leads them to the springs and palm trees of Elim (15:26–27).

Megiddo: A fortress city that witnessed major battles in the history of Israel. It was located on an open plain. John joins the symbols of a battlefield where the innocent are slain (Megiddo) and a mountain (Hebrew: *har*) to form the word Harmagedon (see "Harmagedon"). It symbolises the mountain of Calvary where God was victorious over all evil powers in and through the death and resurrection of Jesus Christ (Rev 16:16–21).

Messianic: The adjective associated with the rule of the Messiah. "Messiah" in Hebrew and "Christ" in Greek mean "the anointed one". The messianic rule and the messianic kingdom are the consequences of God's victory over evil in the death and resurrection of Jesus the Messiah, the anointed and chosen one.

Numbers: John regularly uses numbers to communicate his message. The most important ones are "seven" which means completion, "three" which means perfection, and a play upon seven years, or half of seven years, a "broken" time. Coming from Dan 7:25; 12:7, this number is sometimes represented by forty-two months, 1260 days, or "a time, two times, and half a time". These periods symbolise a time of suffering that will lead to vindication. The number "four", from the four corners of the earth, refers to earth and creation.

Postmillennialism: The belief that Rev 20:1–3 teaches that there will be a golden age of faith on earth before Jesus returns for the final judgment.

Premillennialism: The belief that Rev 20:1–3 teaches that Jesus Christ will return prior to the final inauguration of a thousand years of peace.

Prologue: A passage that begins a long narrative, drama, letter or other form of communication. It is normally used to greet the audience and to provide a summary, and even a key, to what follows.

Prophecy: Normally associated with foretelling future events, the main meaning of "prophecy" for John (and for most of the Bible) is to speak in the name of God. It can sometimes be associated with future events, but John's prophecies are not about the future (as is often supposed). They make known God's saving plan for humankind and for all creation.

Rapture: A widely held sectarian Christian belief that at an unknown time those who are still alive on earth will be gathered with all risen believers and they will all meet the Lord in the air. All others will be "left behind".

Revelation: The translation of the Greek word behind "Apocalypse". Theologically, it suggests a communication about God and God's ways that would otherwise be unknown.

Saints: Almost always associated with Christian saints who have suffered or been slain by Roman authorities, John does not use the expression in this sense. Looking back to the descriptions of the "holy ones" of God (see Dan 7:19–27), he points to those few in Israel's history who lived by the word of God and accepted the messianic promises of the prophets (see Dan 9:4–5). These saints do not have to wait for the final judgment (Rev 20:5–6). They have already been saved by the effects of the death and resurrection of Jesus, slain "before the foundation of the world" (Rev 13:8).

Above: *Woman Clothed with the Sun* by John Collier

Satan: The name of the arch-opponent of God's design, the bringer of all evil into the world. He is the dragon, that ancient serpent who deceives humankind (12:9) and destroys the earth (11:18). For John, he is held in a bottomless pit, except for the final battle that took place at Harmagedon, where he was definitively overcome. He exercises his malicious powers by means of his agents: corrupt political and religious authorities (13:1–18).

Son of Man: An expression found regularly on the lips of Jesus in the four Gospels. In Revelation, the figure of Jesus is rendered as "one like the Son of Man". The expression, with its origins in Dan 7:13–14, refers to a figure who comes through suffering and death to final victory because of unswerving loyalty and obedience to God.

Tachos/tachus: A Greek noun (*tachos*) and an adverb (*tachus*) appear regularly in Revelation. They can refer to a very brief time, "soon", or to the speed with which things happen, "quickly". John uses the words to describe the nature of God's action (quickly), not its timing (soon).

The Lamb: John's favourite expression to refer to Jesus, whose death brought about salvation for humankind. Although from different authors, there is a striking similarity between John's Lamb, and the description of Jesus in 1 Peter 2:18–20: "ransomed … by the precious blood of Christ, like that of a lamb without blemish … destined before the foundation of the world" (see also John 1:29, 36). For John, the figure of the Lamb also carries with it the peaceful innocence of the slain Jesus Christ, over against the destructive violence that accompanies the dragon, Satan and his beastly agents, as they perpetrate universal evil, injuring humankind and the whole of creation.

Woman: John skilfully uses the figure of "the woman" (Greek: *hē gunē*) to present humankind and its options. In 12:1–18, John portrays "the woman" in her original splendour, lost as the son is snatched from her. She falls into the desert. She and her children are caught in the ambiguity of the desert, as Satan's agents pursue them (13:1–18). In 17:1–6, 15–18, "the woman" has made a choice. She is mounted on the beast and is thus destroyed. However, in 21:1–4 "the woman" reappears intimately united to the Lamb as his bride (see also 19:6–8) in the heavenly Jerusalem. She is a symbol of the Christian Church where creation and humankind can realise their potential for wholeness and holiness.

ENDNOTES

1 For a survey of these books and their world, see Sherri Brown and Francis J. Moloney, *Interpreting the New Testament. An Introduction* (Grand Rapids: Eerdmans, 2019), 215–222.

2 Stephen D. Moore, *Untold Tales from the Book of Revelation: Sex and Gender, Empire and Ecology* (Atlanta: Scholars Press, 2014), 1.

3 Timothy Beal, *The Book of* Revelation. *A Biography,* Lives of Great Religious Books (Princeton: Princeton University Press, 2018).

4 Richard Bauckham, *The Climax of Prophecy. Studies in the Book of Revelation* (Edinburgh: T. & T. Clark, 1993), x.

5 G. K. Beale, *The Book of Revelation,* The New International New Testament Greek Commentary (Grand Rapids: Eerdmans, 1999), 97.

IMAGE CREDITS

iStock: cover, p. 3, p. 4, p. 5, p. 8, p. 9 (Saint John the Evangelist monastery at Patmos island in Greece), p. 11, p. 12, p. 15, p. 17 (*Seven Golden Lampstands* by Julius Schnorr von Carolsfeld), p. 18, p. 19, p. 21, p. 23, p. 28, p. 30, p. 31, p. 34, p. 35, p. 36, p. 37, p. 38, p. 39, p. 40, p. 41, p. 42, p. 43, p. 44, p. 45, p. 48, p. 49, p. 52, p. 55, p. 60, p. 61, p. 62.

Wikimedia Commons: title page, p. 7, p. 9, p. 10, p. 13, p. 14, p. 16, p. 20, p. 22, p. 24, p. 25, p. 26, p. 27, p. 29, p. 33, p. 36, p. 37, p. 42, p. 46, p. 47, p. 48, p. 50, p. 51, p. 56, p. 57, p. 58, p. 63.

Also by Francis J Moloney:
A Friendly Guide to Mark's Gospel
and
A Friendly Guide to the Resurrection of Jesus

A BASIC BIBLIOGRAPHY

Beal, Timothy. *The Book of* Revelation. *A Biography*. Lives of Great Religious Books. Princeton, NJ: Princeton University Press, 2018.

Brodd, Jeffrey, and Jonathan Reed, eds. *Rome and Religion. A Cross-Disciplinary Dialogue on the Imperial Cult*. Writings from the Greco-Roman World Supplement Series 5. Atlanta, GA: Society of Biblical Literature, 2011.

Collins, Adela Yarbro. *The Apocalypse*. New Testament Message 22. Wilmington, DE: Michael Glazier, 1979.

Corsini, Eugenio. *The Apocalypse. The Perennial Revelation of Jesus Christ*. Translated & Edited by Francis J. Moloney. Eugene, OR: Wipf & Stock, 2019. Reprint of 1983 edition, with a new Foreword.

Friesen, Steven J. *Imperial Cults and the Apocalypse of John. Reading Revelation in the Ruins*. New York: Oxford University Press, 2001.

Howard-Brook, Wes, and Anthony Gwyther. *Unveiling Empire. Revelation Then and Now*. Maryknoll, NY: Orbis Books, 1999.

Koester, Craig R. *Revelation*. Anchor Yale Bible 38A. New Haven, CT: Yale University Press, 2014.

Moloney, Francis J. *Reading Revelation at Easter Time*. Collegeville, MN: Liturgical Press, 2020.

Moloney, Francis J. *The Apocalypse of John. A Commentary*. Grand Rapids, MI: Baker Academic, 2020.

Resseguie, James L. *The Revelation of John: A Narrative Commentary*. Grand Rapids, MI: Baker Academic, 2009.

Thompson, Leonard L. *The Book of Revelation. Apocalypse and Empire*. New York: Oxford University Press, 1990.

Tonstad, Sigve K. *Revelation*. Paideia Commentaries on the New Testament. Grand Rapids, MI: Baker Academic, 2019.

www.ingramcontent.com/pod-product-compliance
Lightning Source LLC
Chambersburg PA
CBHW061058170426
43199CB00025B/2932